THE ULTIMATE
GOLFER

THE ULTIMATE
GOLFER

RICHARD BRADBEER

AND

IAN MORRISON

ABBEYDALE PRESS

This revised and updated paperback edition printed 2007

ISBN 978-1-86147-191-8

1 3 5 7 9 10 8 6 4 2

Abbeydale Press
an imprint of Bookmart Limited
Blaby Road, Wigston
Leicester LE18 4SE

Printed in Thailand

ACKNOWLEDGMENTS
Step-by-step sequences photographed on location at the Penina Golf Course, Portugal. Thanks to Clare Seddon and Michael Hobbs for their assistance.

PHOTOGRAPHS
Phil Sheldon Golf Picture Library
Michael Hobbs Golf Collection
Sarah Fabien Baddiel, The Golf Gallery, London

PUBLISHER'S NOTE
The instructions in this book assume that the player is right handed.
If you are a left-handed player you should reverse the instructions.

Page 1 Sergio Garcia/ pages 2&3 Ernie Els / above, Sergio Garcia and José María Olazábal at the 2006 Ryder Cup

CONTENTS

Playing the Game

INTRODUCTION 8
Equipment 9

STARTING OUT 19
Aiming the Club 20
The Grip 25
Stance 32
The Swing 38
Warm-Up Exercises 59

THE SHORT GAME 65
Pitching 66
Chipping 75

PUTTING 80
Putting Practice 87

HAZARDS AND DIFFICULT SHOTS 91
Greenside Bunker 92
Fairway Bunker 100
Uphill Lie 104
Downhill Lie 105
Ball below Your Feet 106
Ball above Your Feet 108
High Shots over Trees 110
Low Shots in Bushes 111
Low Shots under Trees 112

FAULTS AND PROBLEM SOLVING 115
Slicing 116
Pulling 119
Hooking 120
Pushing 124
Topping 126
Fluffing 129
Over-swinging 132

ERRORS IN THE SHORT GAME 135
Errors in Pitching 136
Errors in Chipping 141
Errors in Putting 144

Tiger Woods

Rules and Etiquette

Types of Matches 153
Handicaps 156
Rules 158

The World of Championship Golf

Origins and Early Days 166
The Golfing Hall of Fame 174
The Great Women Golfers 200
The Great Tournaments 207
Great Golf Courses 234
Glossary 253
Index 254

PLAYING THE GAME

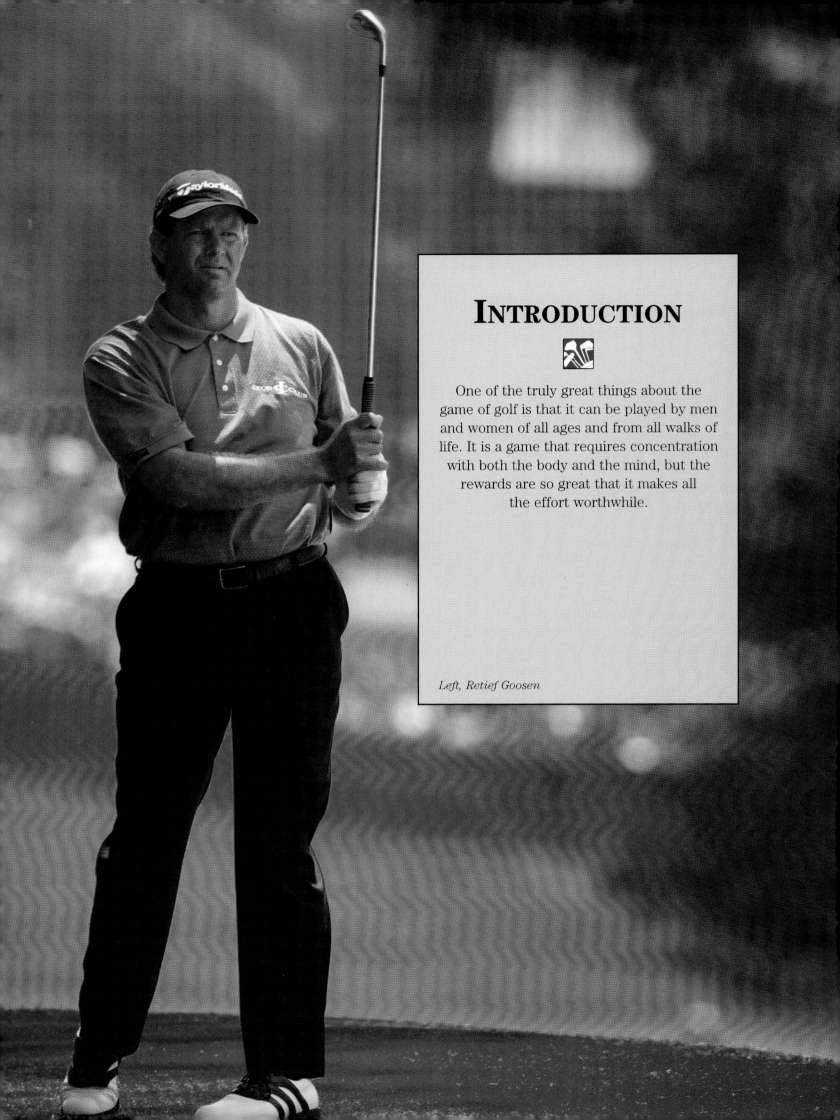

INTRODUCTION

One of the truly great things about the game of golf is that it can be played by men and women of all ages and from all walks of life. It is a game that requires concentration with both the body and the mind, but the rewards are so great that it makes all the effort worthwhile.

Left, Retief Goosen

EQUIPMENT

CLUBS

Golf clubs can now be purchased at many outlets, but it is always best to deal with one that is qualified to give you the correct advice and one you can contact should you have any problems. Value for money does not always mean buying the cheapest clubs and if you deal with the known brands, you will be able to get a comprehensive back-up service.

CLUBS

Top: The current trend is for clubheads with a cavity back. They claim to give a greater sweet spot to strike the ball with. Bottom: A blade-type clubhead.

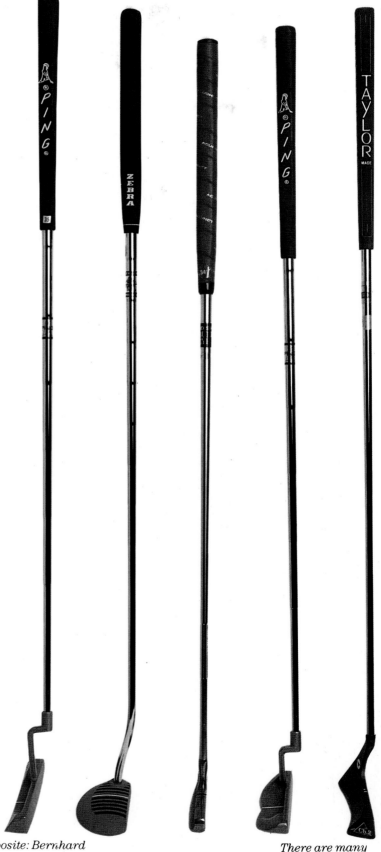

Opposite: Bernhard Langer.

Previous page: Cherry Hills.

There are many different shapes of putter heads; here are several of the most popular.

A Half-set for Beginners

When you first start playing golf it is not necessary to buy all fourteen clubs, seven is sufficient for any new player. A good combination to have would be a 3-wood, 3-, 5-, 7-, 9-irons, a sand wedge and a putter. Alternatively, you could select a 3- and 5-wood, 4-, 6- and 8-irons, a sand wedge and a putter. When buying your first set of clubs it is best to seek the advice of a PGA Professional, as they will be able to help you choose the clubs best suited to your build and physical strength.

Shafts

There are a few points to bear in mind when you purchase new or second-hand clubs. There are many shafts on the market and they can vary a great deal in flex, weight and type. The most flexible shafts 'L' are generally used for ladies' golf clubs, 'R' are used by the majority of men and 'S' by stronger players. Always check that the shaft is correct for your requirements.

A half-set of clubs suitable for a beginner comprising a 3-wood, 3-, 5-, 7-, and 9-irons, a sand wedge and putter.

Two hand-made wooden golf clubs.

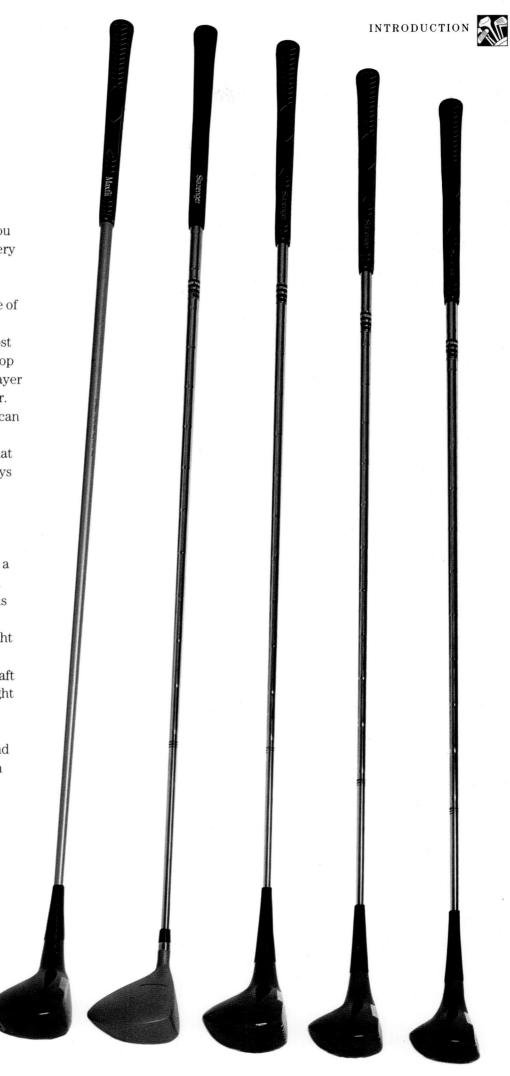

GRIP

As your hands are the only contact that you have with the club the size of the grip is very important. Check that the grip is the right thickness for your hands and that all the clubs in the set have the same grip. The lie of the club should also suit your height.

To help control the hold on the club most people wear a thin leather glove on their top hand – the left hand for a right-handed player and the right hand for a left-handed player.

Shaft flexibility and the size of the grip can effect the swing weight and the overall weight of the club. Again it is important that the weight is right for you, therefore, always try the clubs before you make a purchase.

SWING WEIGHTING

Swing weighting is a method of producing a set of clubs that feels the same when each club is swung. The swing weight of a club is related to the flex in the shaft. The ladies' shaft (L) is fitted to clubs with swing weight C6 to C8, the men's regular shaft (R) is between C9 and D2, and the men's stiff shaft (S) is between D3 and D6. The swing weight can be measured accurately at most professional shops on a swing weight machine. Using the correct flex of shaft and weight of clubs helps to achieve maximum clubhead speed at impact.

From left to right: a no. 1-wood with graphite shaft and head; a metal-headed no. 1-wood with a steel shaft – note the head is larger and designed to give more power; the last three are a set of 1, 3 and 5 persimmon-headed wooden clubs with steel shafts.

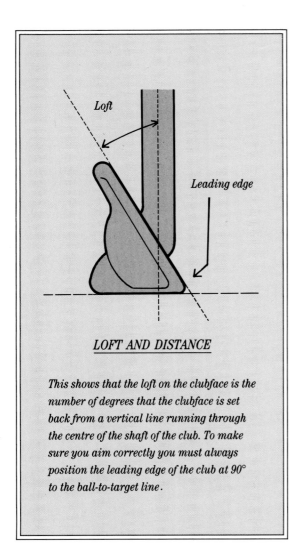

LOFT AND DISTANCE

This shows that the loft on the clubface is the number of degrees that the clubface is set back from a vertical line running through the centre of the shaft of the club. To make sure you aim correctly you must always position the leading edge of the club at 90° to the ball-to-target line.

IRONS	LOFT	LENGTH OF SHAFT In (mm)	APPROX. DISTANCE Yd (ms)
2	18°	38½ (978)	190 (174)
3	22°	38 (965)	180 (165)
4	26°	37½ (953)	170 (155)
5	30°	37 (940)	160 (146)
6	34°	36½ (927)	150 (137)
7	38°	36 (914)	140 (128)
8	42°	35½ (902)	130 (119)
9	46°	35 (889)	120 (110)
Pitching wedge	52°	35 (889)	100 (91)
Sand wedge	58°	35 (889)	80 (73)
WOODS			
1	12°	43 (1092)	240 (219)
2	16°	42½ (1080)	220 (201)
3	20°	42 (1066)	200 (183)
4	24°	41½ (1054)	180 (165)
5	28°	41 (1040)	170 (155)

LOFT AND DISTANCE

You are allowed to have fourteen clubs in your bag when playing golf. Each club serves a different purpose and is used for hitting different distances. This is determined by the loft on the clubface. The lower the number on the sole of the club the less the loft on the face. As the number of each club increases the loft goes up 4°, and the length of the shaft decreases by ½in (12.5mm)

The longest club has less loft, it can therefore hit the ball further, and this is helped by the longer shaft which gives a greater radius to the swing.

As the metal-headed wood gets smaller it also becomes shallower in the face, enabling the clubhead to fit in behind the ball when it is lying on the fairway or rough.

The head on the irons gets larger with a deeper face as the irons get shorter. This enables the club to hit the ball up in the air.

A set of clubs consisting of three metal-headed woods (nos. 1, 3 and 5), and nine irons (nos. 3 to 9, a wedge and a sand wedge) With the addition of a putter and either another wood or iron they would make up the club set.

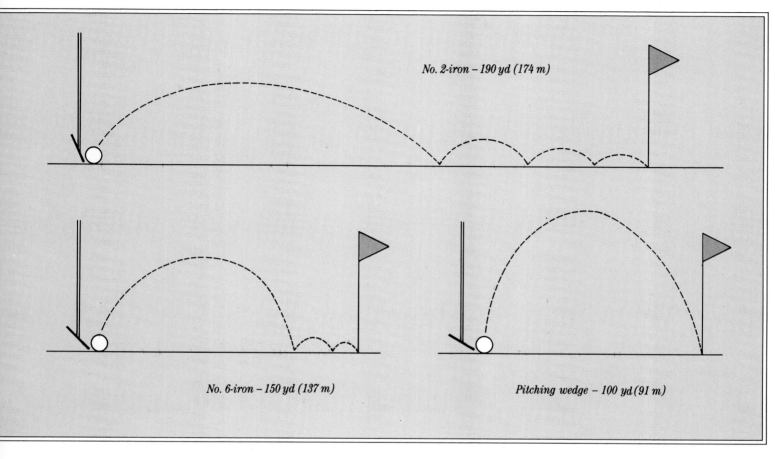

No. 2-iron – 190 yd (174 m)

No. 6-iron – 150 yd (137 m)

Pitching wedge – 100 yd (91 m)

THE GOLF BALL

Golf balls used all over the world are now of universal size – 1.68in (42.5mm) in diameter and weighing 1.62oz (46g). There are basically three types of balls on the market, each varying in the materials used and their performance and durability.

BALATA

Balata is the first choice of low handicap and professional players, who demand maximum feel and spin for control at all times. This ball is made up of a liquid centre, elastic winding and a Balata cover. It is the cover that gives the feel and control that the expert player is looking for. Balata is a natural substance and is not as durable as some man-made materials used in other types of balls.

A ball being wound.

Many golf balls today have club or company logos put on them. Here the balls are being checked before the logo is stamped on.

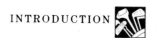

THREE-PIECE BALL

The three-piece ball still gives the feel that professionals are looking for, but it has a different cover making it more durable. The centre of the ball is a rubber-type material which is then wound round with rubber thread. The third part of this type of ball is the cover which in many cases is made of surlyn. This is a ball for the serious golfer who is looking for feel and durability.

A two-piece ball.

This shows the make up of the three-piece ball, starting as a pellet which is rounded and then smoothed and wound round with the rubber thread. The cover which is smooth at this stage, is compressed together and the dimple formation pressed on to the cover. The ball is then sprayed and the logo painted on.

TWO-PIECE BALL

The two-piece ball is probably the most popular ball, giving both distance and durability. It is made up of a solid centre and a man-made cover. Because of its hardness this type of ball, whilst travelling further is often difficult to pitch and putt with.

The dimple pattern on the golf ball varies from one make to another; each manufacturer will of course state that theirs is the best! You should try different types and makes of ball finding out which one suits your type of game. The Balata ball is only made in white but the other two types are made in yellow as well.

Balls being painted.

A two-piece ball. The centre of the ball is rounded and then the granules shown here are made into the cover. The cover is a tough material which maintains its shape. The ball is then sprayed and varnished.

OTHER EQUIPMENT

You will find that tee pegs are either wooden or plastic. It is largely a matter of personal preference which type you choose. One of the other items that you will find useful is a ball marker. These small white discs are used to mark the position of the ball on the green if you have to pick it up. A pitch repair fork is handy for repairing indentations made by the ball on the green.

SHOES

The range of golfing shoes on the market today is enormous and can be rather overwhelming. The deciding factor when buying a pair of golf shoes should be comfort as you have to walk a long way in a round of golf. The main choice to be made is whether to buy spiked or non-spiked shoes. Spikes will give you a better grip, but they are heavier and are not really necessary on the lighter parts of the course. If you do wear spikes be careful not to damage the greens.

A pair of spiked golf shoes.

Golf clubs are still made by hand.

PLAYING IN COLD WEATHER

In cold weather it is tempting to wear several layers of clothing to keep warm. However, this will restrict your swing, so it advisable to select lightweight thermal clothing and a waterproof jacket. The majority of waterproof suits are also wind proof. Large mittens are also an excellent way of keeping your hands warm. Select a pair that are lined and easy to take off for each shot. If your hands get cold you will lose control of the club. Always keep your head covered.

If the weather is severe it is probably worth taking fewer clubs as this will speed up play. Keep checking that the studs in your shoes are not clogged, as this can cause you to slip.

PLAYING IN THE RAIN

When playing golf in the rain you will need to wear outer clothing to stay dry. As with the clothing recommended for cold weather, it is important to select a lightweight waterproof jacket that will not restrict your swing. Umbrellas are also useful for protecting yourself and your equipment from the elements between shots.

One of the greatest hazards of playing in the rain is that if the grip becomes sodden it is extremely difficult to keep firm hold on the club. A clean towel is useful for drying the grip and you can wear all-weather gloves which will enable you to keep a firmer hold. The majority of grips fitted to clubs are made of rubber and you will find that they become less slippery if they are kept clean. The best way to clean them is with a little warm soapy water and a nail brush and then dry them off with a towel. Avoid getting them too wet.

Alternatively many players have their clubs fitted with half or full-cord grips. These grips have cotton thread woven into them which absorbs surface moisture.

It is important to bear in mind that rain gathers on the golf ball which will affect the flight of the ball. Consider using a more lofted club than you would usually, for example, a 5-wood instead of a 3-wood. This will help the ball to become airborne more quickly.

If due to incessant rain your feet sink into the turf at the address your feet will become lower than the level of the ball. To compensate for this move your hands down the grip slightly. if the ground is slippery make sure your shoes are full studded.

Below, Colin Montgomerie shelters from the rain during the 2004 Open Championship at Royal Troon, Scotland.

STARTING OUT

One of the things that you hear so often on the golf course is people saying 'Yes, I play golf, but I am so inconsistent'. Golf is a game that is very much in the mind, and you have to work hard at understanding and mastering the basic requirements for consistent and improving play. Everybody wants results, and results come from a sound routine and knowledge of technique, but they also come from confidence.

Left, Vijay Singh

AIMING THE CLUB

As every shot you play will have a different direction, it is essential to understand how to aim correctly. To ensure that you hit the ball in the right direction you must first be able to imagine the shot you are going to play.

Stand behind your ball to establish the line of flight from the ball to the target – the 'ball-to-target line'. If the target is far away it is easier to start by selecting a point closer to you and in line with the ball and target. Always double-check your aim, and never take it for granted that it is correct.

The part of the club which directs the ball is the leading edge. This must be positioned square to the ball-to-target line and at right angles to your shoulders. This will ensure you have the correct loft on the face of the club.

If the leading edge of the clubface is turned either to the left (a closed face), or out to the right (an open face), this will send the ball off course. Always check the leading edge is square to the ball-to-target line.

THE CLUBHEAD

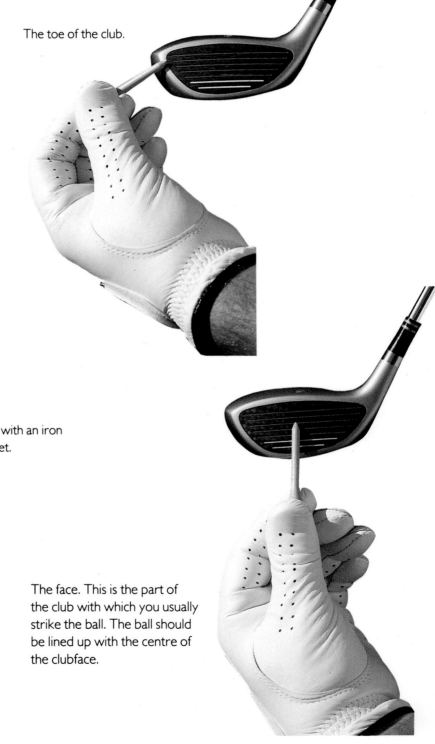

The toe of the club.

The face. This is the part of the club with which you usually strike the ball. The ball should be lined up with the centre of the clubface.

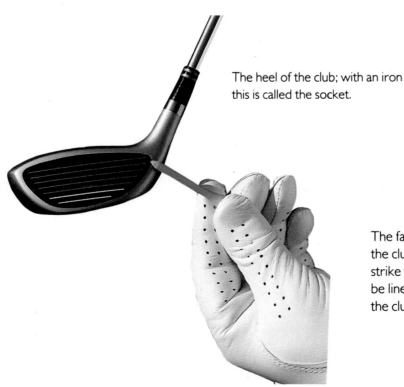

The heel of the club; with an iron this is called the socket.

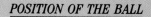

POSITION OF THE BALL

The no. 1-wood is correctly positioned to the ball. The ball should be teed-up so that half of the ball is visible above the clubface. Because clubheads have different depths the amount the ball needs to be teed-up will vary.

LIE OF THE CLUB

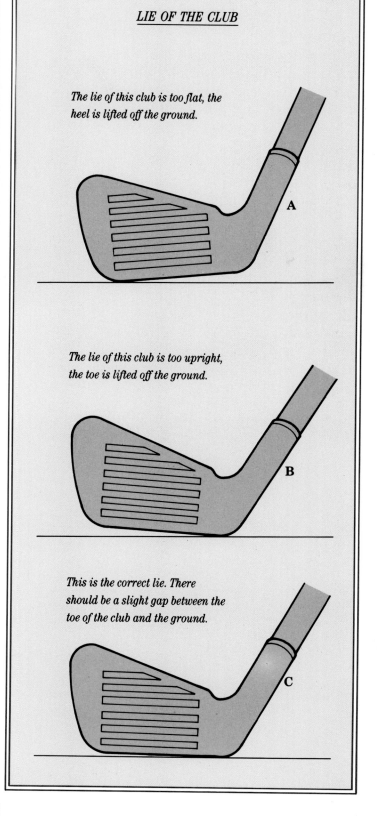

The lie of this club is too flat, the heel is lifted off the ground.

A

The lie of this club is too upright, the toe is lifted off the ground.

B

This is the correct lie. There should be a slight gap between the toe of the club and the ground.

C

The leading edge. Each clubhead is different in shape and loft but they all have a leading edge. The leading edge must be at right angles to your shoulders and square to the target.

OPEN AND CLOSED CLUBFACES

The tees indicate the line to the target
– the 'ball-to-target line'. And here
the 3-wood is set square.

The leading edge is turned to the left,
closing the clubface. This is a frequent
error with this club and should be avoided.

The leading edge is square to the
ball-to-target line.

The toe of the club is turned in,
closing the clubface.

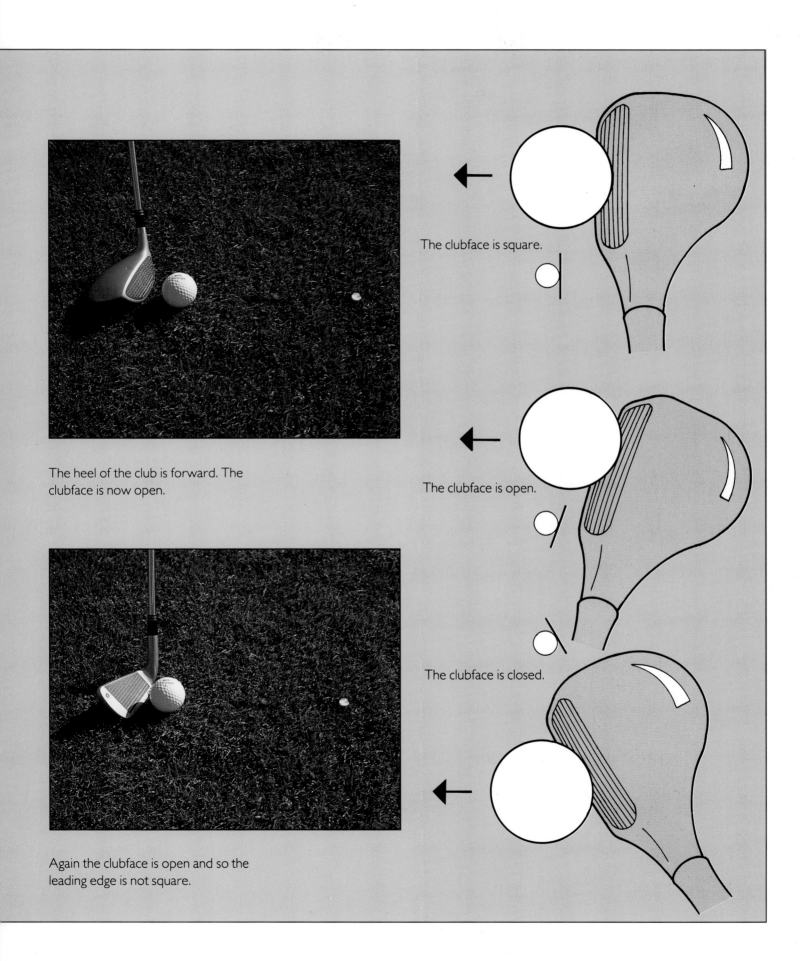

The heel of the club is forward. The clubface is now open.

The clubface is square.

The clubface is open.

The clubface is closed.

Again the clubface is open and so the leading edge is not square.

BALL-TO-TARGET LINE

I Standing behind the ball will help you to establish the ball-to-target line. This is a good exercise to include in your set-up routine.

2 The clubhead is set on the chosen ball-to-target line.

3 Always double-check your aim by looking at the target.

Key Points Card

Points	Remarks
1	Always aim with the leading edge of the golf club.
2	Stand behind the ball looking at the target.
3	Select a point closer to you on the ball-to-target line.
4	Place the clubhead so the ball is in line with the centre of the clubface.

THE GRIP (HOLD)

There are several different ways of holding the club and you should choose the one that feels most comfortable for you. This will largely depend on the size of your hands. Start by learning the correct hold for the left hand. Do not alter the position of your left hand when you place your right hand on the club. The two hands must be trained to work together, as one unit. The following instructions assume that you are a right-handed player. Reverse the instructions if you are left-handed.

THE LEFT HAND

1 Part of the grip should be outside your left hand. This is more comfortable than holding the end of the grip and will help to give more control.

2 The grip of the club should lie diagonally across the palm of your hand approximately ¼ in (6 mm) from the base of your little finger and across to the middle joint of your forefinger.

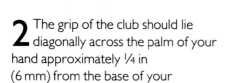

3 When the hand is closed over the grip you should be able to see at least two knuckles on the back of your left hand.

4 The left thumb needs to be just to the right of the centre of the grip. This will form a V-shape with your forefinger which will point between your face and your right shoulder. To ensure this position is maintained in each shot check that the end of the club and your left hand are in line with the inside of your left leg.

THE RIGHT HAND

1 When you place your right hand on the grip make sure you do not move the position of your left hand. The palm of the right hand faces the target. The grip should lie in the middle joints of the first three fingers.

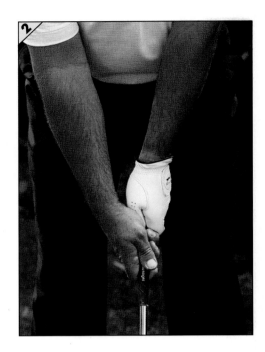

2 The left thumb will now fit inside the right hand as you close your hand over the grip. The right thumb should lie just to the left of the centre of the grip. It should also form a V-shape.

3 Both 'V's must point between your face and right shoulder.

TYPES OF GRIP (HOLD)

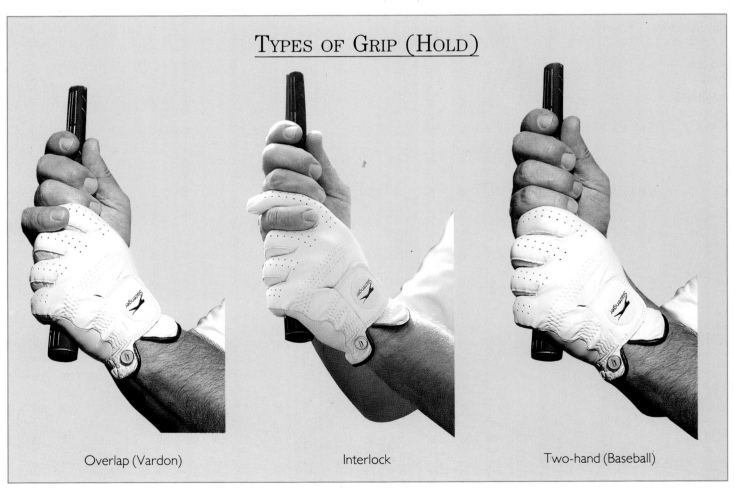

Overlap (Vardon)   Interlock   Two-hand (Baseball)

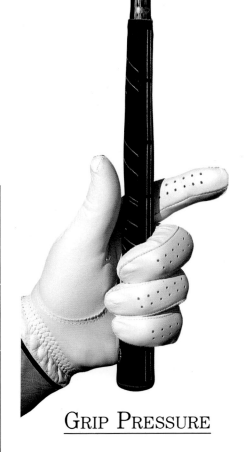

THE PROFESSIONALS

Harry Vardon, c. 1905. The overlapping grip is otherwise known as the Vardon grip because Vardon was considered to be one of the first great players to use this type of hold on the club. This is the most popular of the three grips.

GRIP PRESSURE

1 It is important to maintain the correct pressure on the grip. To control the club at the top of the backswing you need to feel you are holding the club with the last three fingers of your left hand. This gives you control and at the same time enables wrist movement. In your right hand feel the pressure in your middle two fingers.

2 The hands should always be close together to enable them to work as a single unit.

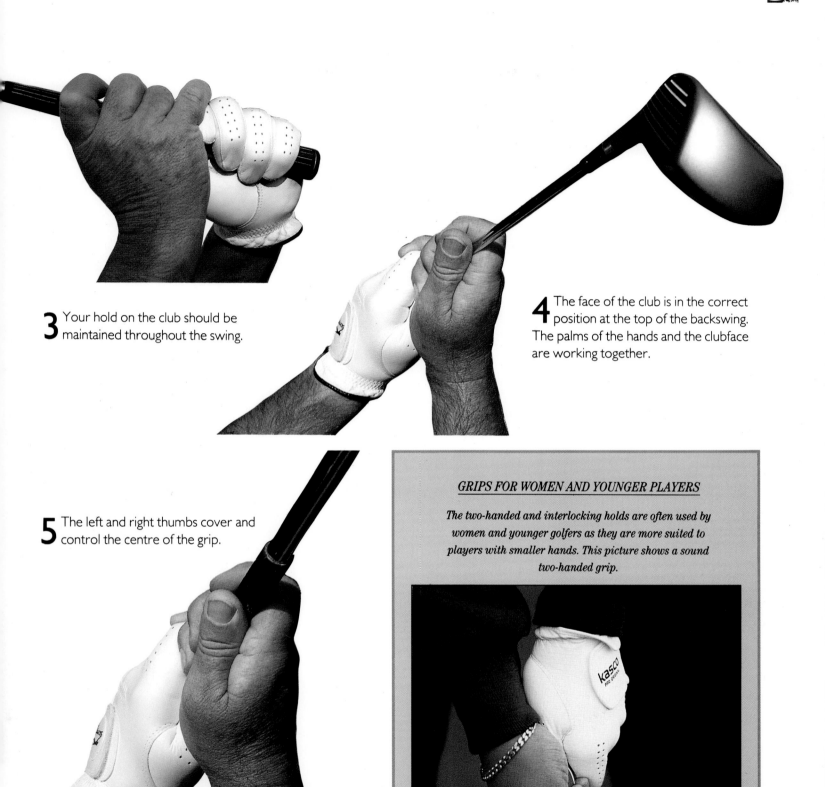

3 Your hold on the club should be maintained throughout the swing.

4 The face of the club is in the correct position at the top of the backswing. The palms of the hands and the clubface are working together.

5 The left and right thumbs cover and control the centre of the grip.

GRIPS FOR WOMEN AND YOUNGER PLAYERS

The two-handed and interlocking holds are often used by women and younger golfers as they are more suited to players with smaller hands. This picture shows a sound two-handed grip.

THE PROFESSIONALS

Arnold Palmer of the USA using the overlapping hold on the club. See how his hands are held high. This was a feature of the great man's play in his heyday. His hands have kept complete control of the club.

COMMON FAULTS

You will often find that if you are having problems with your swing these have occurred because you have the wrong grip. Watch out for the faults shown below and always check you have the right grip.

STRONG GRIP

1 The 'V's formed by the forefingers and thumbs are pointing to the right of the right shoulder. This tends to take loft off the clubface and causes the clubhead to become shut.

Key Points Card	
Points	Remarks
1	*Once you have the correct left-hand grip, do not alter it when you place your right hand on the club.*
2	*Remember the position of the thumbs helps to control the position of the clubface at the top of the backswing.*
3	*Maintain the correct grip pressure. You must not let go of the club during the shot.*

2 See how the face of the club is pointing to the sky, which can result in hooking the ball left, hitting the ball low left or fluffing (hitting the ground before impact with the ball).

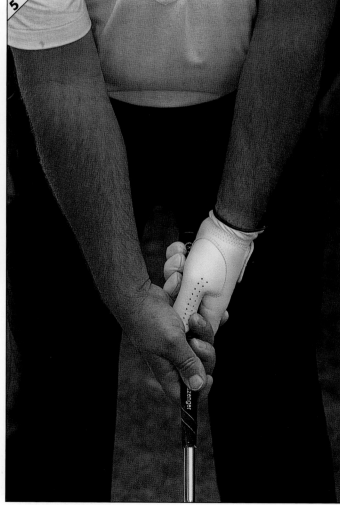

WEAK GRIP

3 & 4 Here the hands are pointing towards the left shoulder. This will increase the loft on the clubface during the backswing and lead to the clubface looking down to the ground. The ball will probably be sliced to the right.

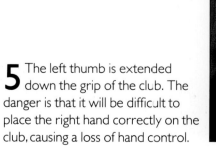

5 The left thumb is extended down the grip of the club. The danger is that it will be difficult to place the right hand correctly on the club, causing a loss of hand control.

STANCE

Having established how to hold and aim the club it is now important to check your posture. Without the correct posture you will find it extremely hard to keep good balance and create the correct movements. Follow the steps shown and in particular note the angle of the spine.

It is largely a matter of personal preference as to how far your feet are apart. This distance will also vary depending on the club you are playing with. But as a general rule your feet should be shoulder width apart when playing with woods and then moved closer together for shorter clubs.

I Relax. Stand with your arms at your sides and feet shoulder width apart.

2 Bend forward from the hips. Your hips should go back and your head and shoulders forward. Keep your back straight.

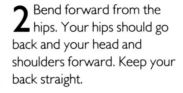

3 Maintaining the same spinal angle, let your arms hang down freely from your shoulders.

BODY ALIGNMENT

1 This now leads us on to body alignment. Shoulders, hips, knees and feet should be square, parallel to the ball.

BODY ALIGNMENT

To obtain the correct alignment to the target imagine a railway line – the clubhead, ball and target are on one rail and your feet, knees, hips and shoulders on the other. This will help you ensure that the clubhead and ball are set square and that you are standing parallel to the target. This is called a square set-up.

2 Holding the club, flex your legs slightly, and let your hands hang down comfortably. Your right forearm will be slightly lower than your left arm. Head neither up nor down.

POSTURE

To help yourself adopt the correct posture follow the routine shown below for every shot you play.

1 First stand upright, check that you have a square set-up – parallel to the ball-to-target line.

2 Keeping your back straight lean forward and flex your legs towards one another.

POSTURE FROM BEHIND

3 Notice how the spine tilts to the right. This should occur naturally if the shoulders are square, with the left hand at the top of the grip.

4 Note how the feet are wider apart now that a longer club is being used.

BALL POSITION

The position of the ball in relation to your feet will vary according to the length of the club. With longer clubs the ball is further forward in the stance (just inside the left heel). As the club gets shorter move the ball back towards the middle of the stance. The ball is also positioned further away from the player when longer clubs are used.

I The body is square to the ball-to-target line.

MEDIUM SHOTS

3 For the medium clubs note how the ball has moved further back in the stance. Its position is more central.

LONG SHOTS

2 Position the ball so it forms a right angle from just inside your left foot to the ball-to-target line. Feet shoulder width apart.

4 As the club gets shorter move your feet closer together. Head still behind the ball.

SUMMARY

In each of the following three pictures the same grip – the overlap – is being used for each type of club. In each case the club is extended from the left arm and the left hand is in line with the inside of the left leg. You can see clearly that both 'V's are pointing between the face and right shoulder. If you looked down the club from this position you would be able to see two or three knuckles on the back of the left hand.

As the club gets shorter then the ball is positioned further back in the stance and the feet move closer together.

LONG SHOTS

1 Ball inside the left foot, feet shoulder width apart, head behind the ball and weight evenly distributed.

MEDIUM SHOTS

2 Ball central in the stance, feet slightly closer together and arms hanging down comfortably.

EXERCISE

This exercise without a club shows the correct hand, arm and body movements for the takeaway. You need the correct posture to do this. Follow through to a point about waist high. From this small movement you can learn the correct co-ordination needed for consistent and improving play.

Short Shots

3 Ball further back in the stance and closer to the player, and slightly more weight on the left leg.

Key Points Card

Points	Remarks
1	*Without the correct posture you will find it extremely hard to remain well-balanced and to swing correctly.*
2	*Timing, rhythm and balance are the key to a good swing.*
3	*Aim, grip, posture, body alignment and ball position have to be correct and consistent to enable you to improve.*

THE PROFESSIONALS

Severiano Ballesteros of Spain is seen here checking his aim before driving. He is using the overlapping (Vardon) grip. His arms are hanging down comfortably from a good posture.

THE SWING

Having mastered the routine for making a good sound address position you are ready to attempt the movements required for the best possible golf swing. The following four series of pictures show the movements for the long (full), medium and short swing. Following this, the separate elements of the swing – grip and ball alignment, the takeaway, the backswing, the downswing and the swing path – are examined in more detail. Remember to check your aim, grip and stance before you start the swing.

THE PROFESSIONALS

Nancy Lopez of the USA playing in England in 1978. This picture shows the complete follow-through which is a feature of a good swing.

THE FULL SWING

I Position the ball level with the inside of the left foot. Stand with a relaxed posture and alignment.

4 Transfer body-weight on to your left side. Release the clubhead to the target with your arms together.

2 The takeaway should be a single movement, with your wrists not cocking before waist height.

3 At the top of the backswing, make a full shoulder turn. The club shaft should be parallel to the target line.

5 Bend your right leg at the knee. Turn your shoulders through, allowing your head to look at the result.

6 At this point your hands should be high and your arms together and well-balanced. Maintain the grip.

THE MEDIUM SWING

1 Position the ball centrally in your stance and stand with your arms hanging down comfortably.

2 Your arms and body should move together but do not cock your wrists until waist height.

3 Keep your head steady and do not take the club as far back in the medium swing as in the full swing.

THE SHORT SWING

1 Note the position of the arms and wrists. You cock your wrists much earlier for the short swing.

2 Take the club up much more quickly, with less left foot and body movement.

3 Don't take your hands much higher than your shoulders. Note the hand and wrist position.

4 As you start the downswing, your legs and arms should work together. Transfer weight on to your left leg.

5 Your head is brought through the swing by your right shoulder.

6 The movement in body-weight should take the left shoe over slightly.

4 Keep your wrists cocked as you start the downswing.

5 Head steady at impact.

6 Balanced follow-through, with your arms together.

WOMEN'S SWING

Even though women have a different physique from men, the same principles of the golf swing apply. They have to control the clubhead and the direction of the down and through swing. However, a good posture is particularly essential to enable the female player to make a good shoulder turn, both on the backswing and follow-through, as well as a good free arm movement.

1 Stand with a good posture, your arms hanging down, body aligned square and legs flexed at the knee.

3 Fold your right arm with your elbow pointing down to the ground, the shaft of the club should be parallel to the ball-to-target line.

2 This picture shows a good one-piece takeaway, with the hands and the clubhead working together.

4 After impact your hands are at waist height, your head should be steady and left arm about to fold.

5 At the end of the follow-through your body should be facing the target and hands high.

THE PROFESSIONALS

Dottie Mochrie of America is seen here clearing the lower half of the body through impact so that the arms and club can be swung towards the target.

GRIP AND BALL ALIGNMENT

The address position is a rehearsal for the impact the clubhead is going to make with the ball. As your hands are your only physical contact with the club their position in relation to the golf ball is very important.

HANDS TOO FAR FORWARD

2 Both hands and the grip of the club are in front of the ball. Looking down the club both hands will be to the left of the ball. This position could cause an early wrist cock.

HANDS TOO FAR BACK

1 Both hands and the grip of the club are behind the ball. Looking down the club at the ball both hands will be to the right of the ball. This could cause the hand action on the takeaway to be too late.

CORRECT POSITION

3 The left hand just covers the inside of the left leg and is in line with the left side of the ball. The palm of the right hand and the leading edge of the golf club are aligned with the back of the ball. This is where the hands and club should be at impact.

RIGHT HAND

1 The palm of the hand should be in line with the back of the ball and facing the ball-to-target line.

2 This shows the position of the hand relative to the ball when holding the grip of the club.

LEFT HAND

3 The back of the left hand should be facing the target and hanging over the left side of the ball.

THE GRIP

5 The hands are in the overlap grip. Both palms are facing one another, and both 'V's are pointing in the same direction.

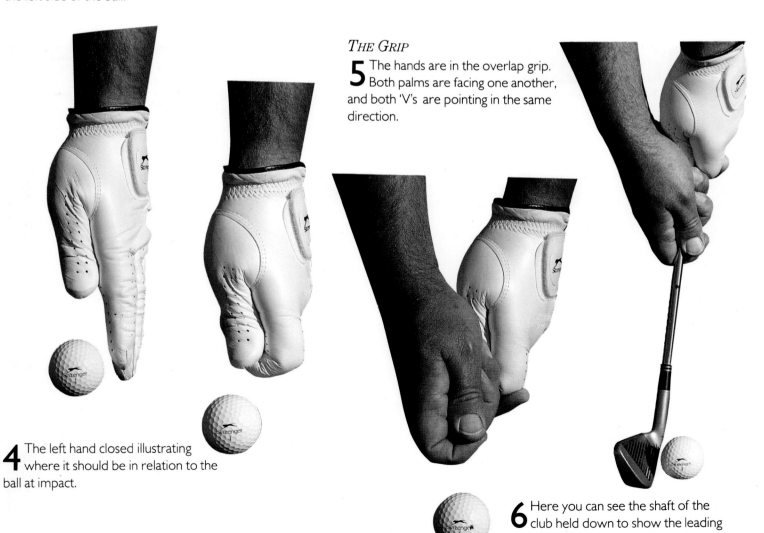

4 The left hand closed illustrating where it should be in relation to the ball at impact.

6 Here you can see the shaft of the club held down to show the leading edge of the club square with the hands.

TAKEAWAY AND BACKSWING

The takeaway is the beginning of the backswing. This must be a one-piece movement, with the left and right sides moving together. Throughout this part of the swing your elbows must remain the same distance apart as they were at the address, and you must keep the head of the club square with your shoulders.

Note the difference in angle that occurs between long and short clubs.

NO. 1-WOOD

1 From the address position, the club, arms, shoulders, hips and legs move as one unit. As the club and arms travel beyond the right side body-weight is transferred on to the instep of the right foot. This should not be a conscious action and must happen smoothly and naturally. The left hand, the back of which was pointing towards the target, will now face away from you.

2 From behind the ball you can see how the arms move together and have stayed the same distance apart as they were at the address. The clubhead, shaft and grip are an extension of the left arm. This unit is parallel with the ball-to-target line.

3 This shows the completed backswing for all long clubs. The shoulders have turned 90° and the hips 45°. The angle of the spine is the same as it was at the address. The hands have kept total contact with the golf club and maintained a square clubface. The left arm is comfortably straight and the right arm bent with the elbow pointing to the ground just behind the right foot.

SHORT IRON

1 The wrists cock sooner at the start
of the backswing with the short iron.
The hands and arms are used to make
the action, rather than the body, enabling
you to maintain the angle set at the
address.

2 Again the left arm and the club on
the ground are in line with one
another. Because the ball is now closer to
you the club will come up at a steeper
angle. This in turn will give a steeper
attack on the ball. Short iron clubheads
are more rounded so when the ball is
struck it runs up the face of the club
causing backspin.

3 At the top of the swing the wrists are
fully cocked at shoulder height. The
head is steady and there is less body
movement than with longer clubs.

4 From a different angle you can see
how there is less body movement.
The hands are controlling the clubface,
the arms are together and swinging
freely from the chest.

LONG AND SHORT CLUBS

1 With the long clubs, the arms and club move without an early wrist action, whereas with shorter clubs the wrists take the club back.

2 Note how the angle you swing the club away from the ball alters with the distance that you stand from the ball.

Key Points Card

Points	Remarks
1	*Make sure the takeaway is a one-piece movement.*
2	*Ensure your body-weight is transferred smoothly on to the instep of your right foot.*
3	*Keep the clubhead square to your shoulders.*
4	*Keep your left arm straight and avoid an early wrist cock when using long clubs.*
5	*Keep your head still, looking at the ball.*

THE PROFESSIONALS

Ernie Els of South Africa is seen here just after impact. His head is held steady and his right leg and foot are transferring weight on to the left side.

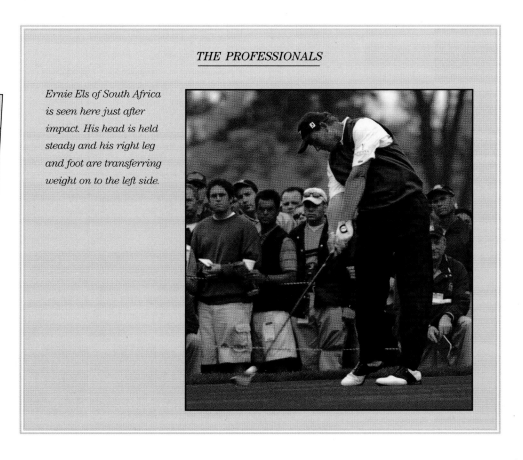

THE PROFESSIONALS

Tiger Woods is one of the world's most exciting players. This picture shows the force with which he hits the ball, allowing the right shoulder and right side to keep moving through impact with his very individual foot action.

EXERCISE

Practice holding the shaft of the club further down. This will help keep the whole club as part of your left arm and work on the shoulder hip and leg movement at the start of the swing. See how when you cock the wrists the handle of the club breaks away from your arm.

THE DOWNSWING AND FOLLOW-THROUGH

The downswing starts from the moment you complete the takeaway of the club and describes the path of the clubhead from the top of the backswing down to the ball on impact. The follow-through describes the path of the club after impact. The club, wrists, arms, body and legs must all work smoothly together so that the clubhead arrives square-on to the ball.

LONG CLUBS

1 The lower part of the body moves towards the target as the arms come down from the top of the backswing with the wrists still cocked. This keeps the head steady and the right shoulder back at the start of the downswing, ensuring the shoulders will be square to the ball-to-target line at impact.

2 The whole of the right side continues to move through impact unrestricted by the head. Note the width of the arc the club has made at this point.

3 Hands high, body well-balanced and spinal angle maintained. This shot will finish just to the left of the centre of the fairway in pole position.

MEDIUM CLUBS

1 With medium length clubs the legs and arms again pull the club down, with the head held steady.

2 The arms and shoulders swing the club through to the target moving underneath the head.

Key Points Card

Points	Remarks
1	From the top of the backswing the club, wrists, arms, body and legs must all work together.
2	Transfer your weight smoothly from right to left.
3	Hit through the ball, keeping your head down and a still body position.
4	Follow through until your hips and body are facing the target.

3 The body is facing the target with body-weight on the left side. See how the divot was taken after impact.

SHORT IRONS

1 With the short iron it is a downward strike. Again, the shoulders are back ready to be square to the target at impact.

2 This is an unrestricted movement through the shot with the left side.

3 The water was no problem because the club had plenty of loft and did not stop on the shot.

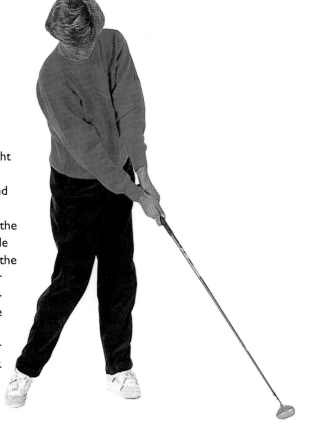

LONG SHOT

The downswing has brought the weight of the body on to the left side; the shoulders are square to the target, and the legs clear the hips to allow the hands and arms to extend and swing the clubhead to the target. With both male and female golfers a good posture at the address is essential to keep the upper half of the body square to the ball-to-target line at impact. Here we see the spinal angle is being maintained to enable the right shoulder to be lower through impact than the left shoulder.

THE PROFESSIONALS

Phil Mickelson is the best left-handed player in the world. He is seen here showing a well-balanced follow-though. The angle of the spine is maintained throughout the shot.

SHORT SHOT

The downswing movements through the legs and hips transfer weight on to the left side and keep the club low to the ground at, and after, impact. The hands, arms and clubhead have moved together through impact.

53

SWING PATH

In the first picture (1) the ground between the player and the golf club is called 'the inside', and the ground on the other side is called 'the outside'. The correct swing path is from 'in-to-square', and 'in' again. This means that the clubhead is taken back on the inside, and after impact the follow-through should continue on the inside.

I The ground between the player and the golf clubs on the ball-to-target line is called 'the inside'.

2 On the takeaway, due to the body pivoting the club travels over the ground called the inside.

3 And onwards to the top of the backswing. This shows a good angle to the backswing.

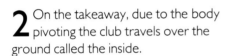

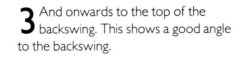

4 This is the important part of swing path. The clubhead comes down to the ball on the inside. It is at this point that the hands release the clubhead to the ball.

5 Through impact, the clubhead is square and the hips are out of the way helping to keep the shoulders square to the ball-to-target line.

6 After impact the body continues to move through to face the target causing the club to swing on the inside.

7 A good extension of the arms takes the club past waist height. The arms are together and body-weight is on the outside of the left shoe.

8 Complete follow-through. The body has moved to face the target and watch the result.

55

SWING PATH

The direction the clubhead is travelling in at impact will govern how the ball will start in its flight. In-to-out and the ball will start right of the target. Out-to-in and the ball will start left of the target. In-to-square and in again and the ball will fly straight.

In-to-out ◀ ◀ ◀ ◀ ◀ ◀ ◀ ◀

Out-to-in ◁ ◁ ◁ ◁ ◁ ◁ ◁ ◁

Ball-to-target line — — — — — —

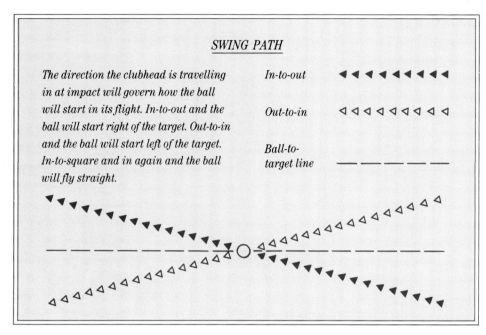

FLIGHT PATH

If the ball swerves in its flight it is because it has side spin on it. This is caused by the position of the clubface at impact, and the swing path. The clubface should be square at impact. Hit with an open face the ball will swerve to the right and with a closed face to the left.

Square

Closed

Open

SWING PATH: EXAMPLE TWO

1 & 2 These two pictures show the club moving towards the target. The head is held steady, shoulders square, weight on the left leg, and right foot moving on to the instep, with the leg bending at the knee helping the hips to clear.

3 & 4 The clubhead is square to the shoulders with the toe of the club having overtaken the heel and beginning to point to the sky. Note the position of the right arm and how the left forearm and elbow are helping to keep the arms together. The head is sti l.

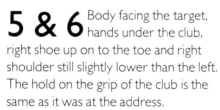

5 & 6 Body facing the target, hands under the club, right shoe up on to the toe and right shoulder still slightly lower than the left. The hold on the grip of the club is the same as it was at the address.

SWING PATH: EXAMPLE THREE

1 Address all set. Shoulders square. See how the arms are hanging down and the back is straight and tilted over the ground. Head clear of chest.

2 Moving down on the inside this is a good swing path. Hips clearing and shoulders ready to move squarely through impact.

3 Notice the divot is square with the line-up and that the club is now travelling over the inside.

4 The follow-through is complete. The angle of spine is the same as for the address. The divot has gone to the left of the target, indicating the clubhead moved from square to the inside, through impact.

WARM-UP EXERCISES

ARMS AND HANDS

It is essential in the playing of all golf shots that you maintain your hold on the grip of the club. To enable you to do this from the start warm up before you play. This exercise will give you a stretching feeling in your arms and also rehearse the action of the arms for the backswing. Repeat this exercise several times. Then repeat the movement in the same way but taking the club to your left side. While you are doing this feel the pressure of your hold on the club in the last three fingers of your left hand and practise maintaining it throughout the action.

1 Stand in the address position.

2 Standing upright, lift the club up above your head and between your right shoulder and the right side of your head. Keep your arms the same distance apart at the elbows as they were in the address position.

3 Repeat this action for the left side, lifting the club up between your left shoulder and left side of your head.

SHOULDERS

These movements are designed to help you understand and practise the correct shoulder movements and angle of the spine.

1 Hold the golf club in front of you, across your chest. Assume the correct posture.

2 Keeping your head still, turn your shoulders so that the grip points outside your right shoe. The hips and legs also respond to this shoulder turn. It is important to train yourself to turn around the spine position set at the address, for it is the spine that gives the tilt to the shoulder turn.

3 From the backswing position, keeping your head still, transfer your weight with a leg and hip movement. Bring your shoulders down and around to complete a follow-through position. Notice that the head of the club is now well past the left shoe showing the shoulder turn on the follow-through is greater than that on the backswing. Note how this shoulder movement turns your head so that it is looking along the ball-to-target line.

HIPS

Both the shoulder and hip actions are essential to give the arms and hands the correct angle of attack on the golf ball. Repeat these hip movements several times. The main point to note here is that the hips turn on a line parallel to the ground.

1 Hold the club so that the shaft is parallel to the ground. Set your body in the correct posture for the address position.

2 Keeping your head still, turn your body with the golf club parallel to the ground. This practises the correct hip turn on the backswing.

3 Here you can see the hip and leg action on the follow-through. During this action you should turn your hips rather than tilting them.

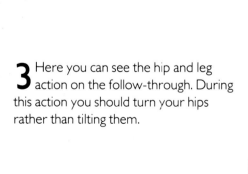

THE SWING

The golf swing is a series of movements, not least of all of the golf club itself. Although people say let the club do the work in fact the club can do very little on its own, and this final exercise will help you accelerate the movement of the club.

For many right-handed golfers it may take some time and effort, to train the left arm and hand to make these movements, as it will for left-handed golfers with the right arm, but in time you will be able to achieve these positions. Being able to understand and perform them is of great importance if you are to play golf to your full potential.

I Hold any club quite far down the grip and roughly in the centre of the stance but with your right hand only.

2 Take the club back a short distance, note how the right arm bends at the elbow.

3 Now swing the club with your hand and arm across your shoulder line as fast as you can. Maintain your hold on the grip of the club. This should give you the feeling of releasing the clubhead past your body. Repeat this action several times. The reason for holding the grip of the club in the middle is that it ensures you do not hit the ground.

5 Swing the club back a short distance with your left arm and hand, and then accelerate the club across your shoulder line as fast as you can while maintaining your hold on the grip. Again you do not want to hit the ground. Notice how the left arm bends at the elbow and also the shape of the clubhead at this point.

4 Next hold the grip of the club with your left hand. Position the club in the centre of your stance.

EXERCISE

This exercise is an aid to showing you, through sound, at which point you should be making the club accelerate. Take any club; hold it the wrong way around. Make a full back and through swing as if hitting a ball. The shaft and grip will make a swishing sound as the club is swung down and through. The noise should occur at and after the area of impact.

6 Again this should give you the feeling of releasing the clubhead and shaft past your body.

STRETCHING

1 Taking two or three clubs with similar lengths of shafts, set up for the address position. Do not use a ball. Because you are using more than one club you will not be able to create a correct hold on the club, but make sure that you can control how far the clubs go back on the backswing and the follow-through.

2 & 3 Make this full swing as shown here, avoid hitting the ground as you swing through. The weight of the clubs will help you in stretching the arm and shoulder movement.

Opposite: Ian Woosnam

THE SHORT GAME

Having learnt the basics of the game of golf, it is important to adapt these skills so that you can play shots from different parts of the course. Greenside shots may require either a short high ball, the pitch, or a low, running ball, the chip. The pitch requires a lofted club to lift up the ball over a hazard, while the chip requires a straighter-faced club so that the ball flies away on a lower trajectory.

Right, Ernie Els

PITCHING

The pitch is used when you need the ball to fly high in the air over a hazard, such as a bunker or a bank. A lofted club – the sand or pitching wedge – is used to give the ball lift. Your choice of club will depend on the lie of the ball and the distance to the target. The pitching wedge is the more versatile of these two clubs because the sand wedge must only be used in a bunker or on a soft, grassy lie. You can also vary the strength of the pitch by how far down the grip you hold the club.

The pitch is what is called a 'pressure' shot because it is a chance for you to improve your score. If you fail to send the ball high it may also end up in a bunker!

2 Here you can see the distance from the ball to the target. With the bunkers in the way the ball must go in the air.

3 Use the full length of the club for this shot. Check the club and ball are lined up to the target, the flag. Nothing is in the way of the swing path – the shoulders are square with the feet, legs and hips open.

I Set the leading edge square. Position the ball slightly off centre, closer to the heel of the club. Stand with the left foot back to give an open stance.

4 Turn your shoulders and legs slightly for the swing but the main action is in your hands and arms. Keep your head quite still and make sure your hands and the clubface are in shape together.

5 This shot was a ball-and-turf contact, caused by the shift in body-weight and the hands and arms hitting down and through at impact.

7 Move on to the instep of your right foot, helping your hips through. The loft of the club is still in view.

6 At impact shift your weight on to the left side, clearing the hips. With your shoulders still square, your arms and golf club send the ball to the flag.

8 Watch the result with the club pointing directly at the flag.

THE SHORT PITCH

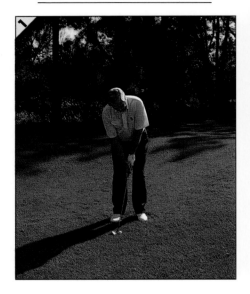

1 If the ball is lying in nice soft grass use the sand wedge. Maintain the same grip as before but position the ball slightly further back in the stance. This picture gives the impression that the hands are ahead of the ball but in fact the left hand is still in line with the inside of the left leg. Put more weight on the left leg and stand with feet, hips and legs slightly open.

2 Take the club back with an early wrist cock, supporting the movement with your shoulders. There should be very little movement of your left leg and hips. The whole of the face of the club is visible.

3 At impact your left arm, the shaft and head of the club return in to line, as they were at the address position. Transfer your body-weight over to the left side, to help keep the clubhead low through the shot. It is essential to keep your head still and shoulders square.

4 The right side should move under your head and shoulders allowing your arms to swing the club to the target. The arms and the whole of the club work together. It is the shape of the clubhead that gives the ball height and direction.

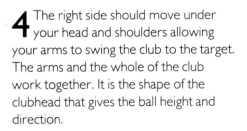

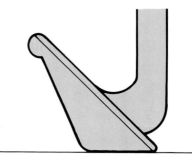

PITCHING

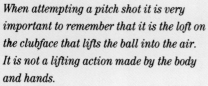

This is how the sole of the pitching wedge sits on the ground.

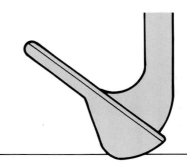

The leading edge of the sand wedge is off the ground. The back of the sole is rounded to give the bounce you need to move enough sand to get the ball out of the greenside bunker.

When attempting a pitch shot it is very important to remember that it is the loft on the clubface that lifts the ball into the air. It is not a lifting action made by the body and hands.

In the first picture the leading edge is square to the ball, presenting the correct loft on the clubface. On the takeaway and backswing the body stays still as the wrists and arms take the club back and up.

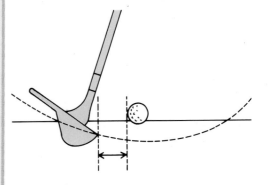

The distance between the ball and the club should be between 1½ and 2 ins (35–50 mm)

A Short High Lob Shot

1 When addressing the ball for a short, high, lob shot to a raised green your legs should be more flexed at the knee. Position the ball quite close to your feet and not too far back in the stance.

3 Keeping your head steady, but in no way forced down, make a smooth transference of weight on to your left side with your feet, legs and hips. The clubhead should still be extended from the shoulders.

2 Just before impact keep your wrists cocked and pull the club down to the ball with your arms and body-weight.

4 Follow through with your right shoulder lower than your left. Your head should naturally turn to face the target. Notice that the loft can still be seen on the face of the club.

5 Watch the result from a well-balanced position.

THE PITCHING WEDGE

The pitching wedge is a very versatile golf club which is used to play high shots to the green from many different distances.

In the series of pictures on the following page note that the distance of the ball from the feet slightly increases as the length of the shot increases, and the arms and shoulders swing the club back further as the shot being played gets longer.

In each case the hands and arms are working together to create a square impact. The head is held steady and the weight of the lower body moves on to the left side, with shoulders becoming square to the ball at impact. The angle of the spine is maintained through impact and as the shot being played gets longer the clubhead is released in a slightly different way. The extent that the body moves through the shot increases with the longer pitching wedge shots.

To learn just what you can achieve with the pitching wedge you need to spend time playing shots of varying distances. Find out how much arm-swing and body movement you personally have to make to hit the ball different distances. Always watch the results. You must learn to play all these shots from memory which will require a sound technique and plenty of practice.

Striking with the pitching or sand wedge is what is called a ball-turf-contact. This is achieved with the correct movements of the lower body-weight, and the arms and club on the downswing and through impact. It is very important that you do not let the club overtake your arms as you hit the ball. You must never try and lift the ball off the ground up into the air, use the loft on the clubface.

This series of pictures illustrate the changes that occur in the swing as the player moves further back from the target. In each case the club is swung further back as the shot being played gets longer.

PITCHING WEDGE SHOTS FROM
DIFFERENT DISTANCES

In each of the four series of pictures the player is further away from the target. Notice how the distance that the club is swung back and the extent the body moves through the shot increase with the longer shots.

THE PROFESSIONALS

*Nick Faldo of England playing a pitch up and over a bank to the green.
The clubface has still got loft on it. Notice how he is not wearing a glove
on his left hand. Many of the best players remove their glove for pitching,
chipping and putting.*

CHIPPING

This is a shot played from various distances from the putting surface when you need a low running ball, rather than a high ball. You can use your putter for this shot but often the fairway or the approach to the green is too wet, or not smooth enough, to roll the ball over. The ideal club loft for this shot is a 4-iron, but as the shot is played with the ball positioned quite close to your feet and the 4-iron shaft is quite long it might get caught up in your clothing. To avoid this occurring use a 6- or a 7-iron.

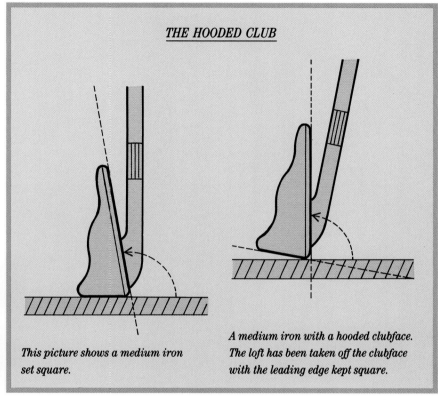

THE HOODED CLUB

This picture shows a medium iron set square.

A medium iron with a hooded clubface. The loft has been taken off the clubface with the leading edge kept square.

1 When you set the leading edge square your hands should be a little ahead of the ball, this has the effect of taking loft from the face of the club, so that it is not closed but hooded. Position the ball slightly back in the stance and stand with your body-weight a little more on the left leg than on the right. Notice how close the ball is to the feet.

2 Move your arms, hands and club back together with no wrist break, keeping the clubhead low to the ground. The clubface should still be hooded.

3 Just before impact the clubhead and shaft, and hands and arms, should return to the same position as in the address. Keep your body very still.

4 As you follow through your wrists should not move and you should keep the body quite still. The ball will fly away low to the ground.

5 Move your arms and club towards the target as one unit. Take them forward at least as far as they went back on the backswing. During this action keep your legs still and shoulders square.

6 Watch the result.

CLOSE TO THE
PUTTING SURFACE

1 Look at the spot where you would like the ball to land and then run up to and in the hole.

2 Set the ball quite close to your feet and hold the grip of the club quite low down. Body-weight just slightly more on your left side which will help keep the clubhead low through impact.

3 The action is a movement of the hands and arms, not the body. The clubhead should still be hooded and low to the ground.

4 Swing your arms and club together so that impact is slow and smooth. Keep your body still and shoulders square to the ball-to-target line.

5 The clubhead should remain low to the ground as it moves towards the target. Do not cock your wrists. Keep your body and head still.

6 Follow through at least as far forward as you went back on the backswing. The ball is running towards the target.

1 Hold the grip of the club slightly further up than for the other chipping shots to help make a longer backswing. Feet, legs and hips open.

CHIPPING FROM FURTHER AWAY

2 Cock your wrists in order to swing the club further back and hit the ball a greater distance. Little to no body movement.

3 Bring the clubhead into the ball low to the ground. Note the movement of the right leg.

4 Your club, hands and arms should be working smoothly together with your right leg and side moving towards the target. Some grass will be moved at impact.

5 Watch the result with the clubhead and the ball still in line with one another. The ball is low and ready to run.

Key Points Card

Points	Remarks
1	*Always use the correct hold on the club.*
2	*Select the correct club and decide where you want the ball to land on the green.*
3	*Keep the body still during the shot.*
4	*Use little to no wrist action.*
5	*Keep the clubhead low to the ground.*
6	*Swing the club backwards and forwards the same distance.*

THE CHIP SHOT

The chip is a low running shot, therefore you need to take loft off the clubface. Select a club that has a comfortable length of shaft. At the address set your hands slightly ahead of the ball, this will deloft the club. The clubface is now hooded.

On the takeaway, there is no wrist break, the clubhead is still hooded, the body stays steady and the clubhead is low to the ground.

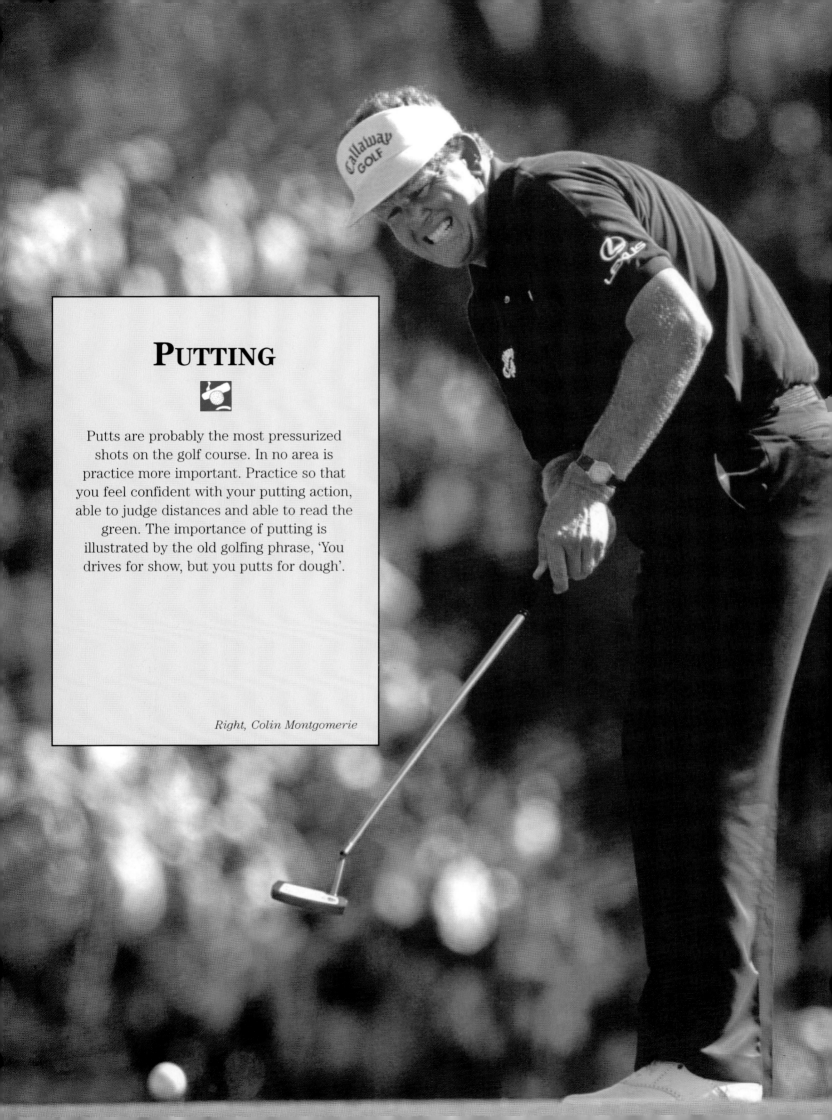

PUTTING

Putts are probably the most pressurized shots on the golf course. In no area is practice more important. Practice so that you feel confident with your putting action, able to judge distances and able to read the green. The importance of putting is illustrated by the old golfing phrase, 'You drives for show, but you putts for dough'.

Right, Colin Montgomerie

PUTTING

Putting is an area of the game that is neglected by many club and higher handicap players. This may be because the green is an accessible part of the golf course and if you fail to putt the ball then 'all the world' can see. Very few people are prepared to spend time on the practice green and practise is what is usually required.

Concentration and confidence play a big role in all golf shots, and at no time are they more important than when putting. You only have to watch how much time and care the professional players put into the preparation of their shots on the putting green to see how much concentration is required. Confidence will come from good sound technique and practice. Always remember that however close you are to the hole, do not trust to luck. Take care to line up for the shot. Putting is never as easy as it looks.

I The putter head is set square to the target with the ball in the centre of the clubface. A reverse overlap grip is being used and the arms are extended down. Ball positioned just left of centre in the stance, the body is evenly balanced. Head positioned over the ball.

2 At the takeaway the head and body are kept still as the club is taken back with a movement of the arms and shoulders. Try and avoid using wrist action when putting. Move the whole of the putter – the head, shaft and grip – with a pendular movement of the arms.

3 On the follow-through the head and body are kept still, and the whole club swung with the arms, using no wrist break. How far the putter is taken back and through will depend on the length of the putt and the speed of the green.

Opposite: Jack Nicklaus.

BALL ALIGNMENT

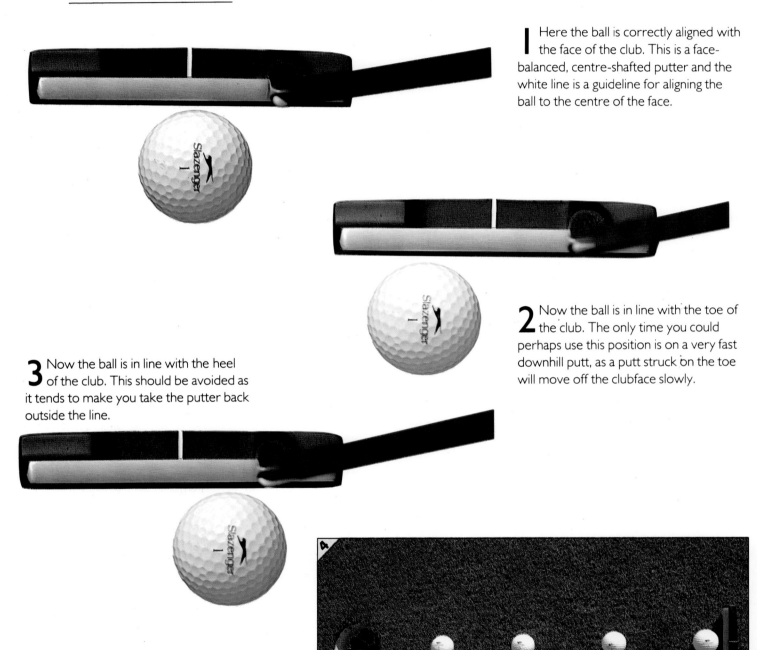

1 Here the ball is correctly aligned with the face of the club. This is a face-balanced, centre-shafted putter and the white line is a guideline for aligning the ball to the centre of the face.

2 Now the ball is in line with the toe of the club. The only time you could perhaps use this position is on a very fast downhill putt, as a putt struck on the toe will move off the clubface slowly.

3 Now the ball is in line with the heel of the club. This should be avoided as it tends to make you take the putter back outside the line.

4 This line of balls indicates how you should imagine the ball moving off the face of the putter and rolling in to the hole. As in all shots aiming is very important.

THE GRIP

1 Put both hands close together, with thumbs on the top of the grip and the index finger of your left hand outside the middle three fingers of your right hand. The index finger of the right hand should go down the grip.

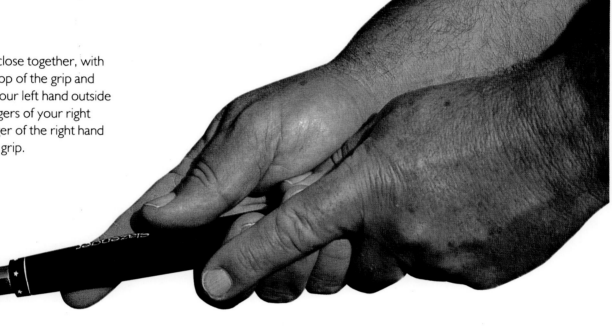

2 A different view of the hands. This is called the reverse overlap grip and it is just one of many ways you can hold the putter. Whichever way you hold the putter you must make sure it becomes part of your arms because a good putting action avoids independent wrist movement. The pressure of the grip should be quite soft so that you feel you are moving the head with your arms and shoulders.

3 Holding the head over the hole like this shows that the face of the club is square to the target, the hole.

PUTTING

THE ADDRESS

It is important to keep the body out of the way to enable free movement of the putter back and through. The ball is in line with the inside of the left shoe which will help to create top spin and make the ball roll. Your head should be directly over the ball and hands held away and out from the legs. This helps to cut down the use of the wrists. Body-weight well-balanced as you will be standing still throughout the stroke.

THE PROFESSIONALS

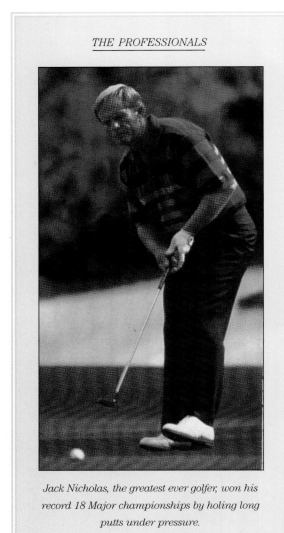

Jack Nicholas, the greatest ever golfer, won his record 18 Major championships by holing long putts under pressure.

BALL-TO-TARGET LINE

View from behind the line of the putt. The line of the feet and body is square with the ball-to-target line.

THE SHORT PUTT

The putt shown here is a good length to practise with. Given that putting is largely a question of confidence it is often better to practise with putts that you are likely to hole rather than destroying your confidence by missing longer ones.

I Hold the grip and check that the 'V' of your left hand is pointing to your left shoulder and that the 'V' of your right hand is pointing to your right shoulder. This will help keep your arms and hands together as one unit. Remember that for the putt the address position is well-balanced and that the ball lines up with the inside of your left shoe.

2 In the short putt take the putter low to the ground as one unit from your shoulders. The distance that the putter goes back will depend on the length of the shot and the speed of the green.

3 On contact do not create any wrist movement. Keep the clubhead low with the face at right angles to the ground. Your head position should stay very still and there is no leg or hip movement.

4 On these short putts it is tempting to look at the hole as you stroke the putt, but continue concentrating on the shot.

THE LONG PUTT

1 During the set-up for the longer putt think of the distance you have to roll the ball for it to reach the hole.

2 After impact keep your head still, stroke the ball smoothly towards the hole with the arms and club.

3 Even when the golf ball is halfway to the hole your head should still not have moved.

4 The only change in these two pictures has been the movement of the ball. The head has stayed still.

5 View of the follow-through. The putter reaching completion.

Key Points Card

Points	Remarks
1	*Check you have the correct grip.*
2	*The ball should be aligned to the centre of the clubface.*
3	*The face of the club should be square to the target.*
4	*Putting is a shoulder and arms movement. There should be no wrist action during the stroke.*
5	*Keep your head still.*

PUTTING PRACTICE

It is always best to practise on a level part of the green; once you can make the ball race straight on short distances then you will be able to cope with long putts and borrows in the greens.

The most important part of any putt is the first 9–12 ins (230–300 mm). If the shot starts correctly there is a good chance of success, but a putt that starts badly rarely improves.

Having lined the ball with the centre of the clubface practise making a smooth back and through swing striking the ball in the same spot – that is the spot on the clubface that you lined the ball up with at the address.

Depending on the speed and the length of the green the distance you have to swing the putter back will vary. For putts of up to 5–6 ins (125–150 mm) the putter head needs to go back in a straight line from the ball and hole. As the length of putt increases the length of the swing will also increase and in so doing the putter will come back slightly on the inside.

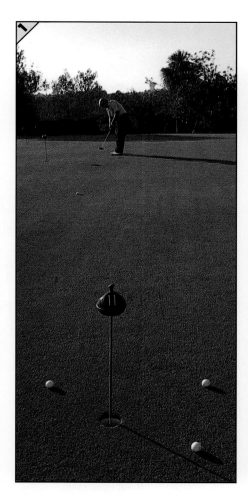

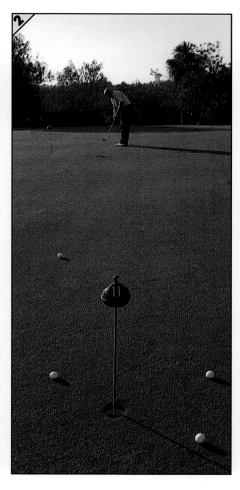

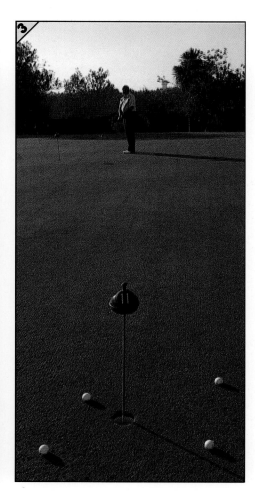

1 You do not need a hole to practise this exercise. Take four balls and play the first one to an open area.

2 Repeat the same putt three or more times, get the four balls to finish as close to one another as possible.

3 This exercise will help you practise the pace of the green and develop a consistent stroke.

HOLING SHORT PUTTS

Place four balls each a little further from the hole. Hole them, working from the one nearest to the hole. Start by testing yourself on a short putt and gradually move the balls further away.

SHAPING THE PUTT

The amount you have to allow for borrows on the greens will depend on the texture of the grass, which in turn determines the speed of the green. The golden rule is that if you decide that you have to allow for the ball to move left or right because of the lie of the land, then you must endeavour to set the ball moving straight from the putter head and let the ground shape the putt. If the surface of the green is fast then you need to allow more into the borrow.

Always look from behind the ball to see what shape the putt is going to make. If you are undecided then take a look at the putt from the hole back to the ball. On a downhill putt you will always see the line more clearly from the hole to the ball. When the putt is uphill have a good look from the side of the putt. This will give you a better view of the slope you are about to negotiate.

Key Points Card

Points	Remarks
1	Start by practising short putts to build up your confidence.
2	Repeat the same length of putt several times to develop a consistent stroke.
3	Then practise putts moving further away from the hole each time.
4	If there are borrows in the green let the ground shape the putt.

THE ELEMENTS OF PUTTING

Address the ball with the face of the putter at right angles to the ground and the ball in line with your left heel. Strike the ball with an upward movement to cause top spin and roll. Keep the putter head quite low to the ground as it passes the left shoe. Having set your line and address you must stand quite still and stroke the ball and make it roll.

Opposite: Greg Norman.

HAZARDS AND DIFFICULT SHOTS

However good you are at golf there are bound to be times when you will find yourself in an awkward situation, whether it is under some trees, on a slope or in a bunker. In these cases it is often best not to be too ambitious, and you should concentrate on the job in hand – getting your ball back on to the fairway. Once there you can think about your next shot.

Right, Ernie Els

GREENSIDE BUNKER

1 Feet, legs, hips and shoulders open to the target. Position the ball just left of the centre in your stance. This will help you to present the full loft of the club to the target. Settle your feet in the sand, this will give you a firm stance and help you feel its consistency. Look at the sand about 2 in (50 mm) behind the ball. Because of the open stance a little more of your lower body-weight will be on your left leg. Use the standard hold on the club so that the clubface is open to your stance.

2 Take the club back and up with your hands and arms, and a responding shoulder, hip and leg movement. The amount of movement required will depend on how far you have to hit the shot. Notice how the club that is swung back is pointing in the same direction as the club aligned along the feet. This indicates that the golf club should move along the line of the address position.

3 At the start of the downswing the clubhead has lots of loft and the face is visible. With this alignment and arm-swing, your swing should naturally go across the ball-to-target line. Keep your hands and arms together, working underneath the golf club.

4 Make contact with the sand about 2 in (50 mm) behind the ball. Head position very still. Move your legs and hips out of the way to help your shoulders keep the line they were set in at the address. The ball will move left of the target along the swing path of the club. But because you aimed the clubface at the target, and open to your stance, the ball will cut in its flight.

5 Your right leg, hip and shoulder move to help take the swing high on the follow-through. Keep your hold on the club and continue to swing along the open line set by your body at the address.

Key Points Card

Points	Remarks
1	Use a sand wedge with bounce.
2	Ball forward in the stance.
3	Look at the sand where you intend to hit.
4	Swing along the open shoulder line.
5	Follow through keeping loft on the clubface.

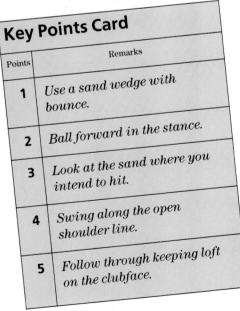

GREENSIDE BUNKER: EXAMPLE TWO

1 Ball slightly forward and clubhead above the sand.

2 This shows the swing of the hands and arms taking the club back and up.

3 Body swinging under the head, arms extended with the hands keeping the loft on the face of the club.

4 Hands held high with the shoulders just bringing the head around.

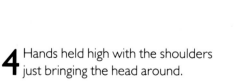

5 Body pointing left of the target with a full follow-through.

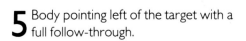

BALL BACK IN GREENSIDE BUNKER

1 Set the ball slightly left of centre in the stance and perhaps a little further away from your feet. Align your body to the left of the target.

2 Swing the club further back, making a fuller hip and shoulder turn. Make sure your arms and legs are working well together on the downswing. Wrists still cocked, head very still with plenty of room for the shoulders to move.

3 Less sand is taken. Your wrists and hands bring the loft of the club through the ball to send it high enough to cover the full distance of the sand.

4 Notice the high follow-through. Keep the top of your body tilted over the ground.

5 Turn your body completely to face to the left of the target and maintain your balance.

FRONT OF GREENSIDE BUNKER: BALL SAT DOWN

1 Stand in a relaxed address position, feet slightly open, shoulders square, the clubhead square to your shoulders and do not hold the club too tightly.

2 Take the club back with your hands and arms, with a little movement coming from your shoulders and hips.

3 Swing down to hit the sand several inches behind the ball. It is likely that your hold on the club will tighten a little at this point.

4 Again head steady. You will hit lots of sand, but keep your arms and hands moving ahead of the golf club. This will ensure you do not turn the club over as you hit the sand.

BALL ON FIRM SAND IN GREENSIDE BUNKER

1 This shot will need a smooth full swing, not taking very much sand.

2 Take the club back without such an early wrist break. This will help get a shallower attack on the sand.

3 Relaxed body and arm-swing to the top of the backswing.

4 Slip the club under the ball slowly.

5 Good release of the clubhead.

6 Make a relaxed full follow-through.

BALL ON THE UP-SLOPE OF GREENSIDE BUNKER

1 Position the ball slightly to the left of centre in the stance. Set your body perpendicular to the slope. To achieve this you will need to widen the stance and flex your knees into the slope.

2 As with all these bunker shots keep your head steady.

3 Maintain your balance and the angles set at the address. Take the club back and up with your hands and arms.

4 Your legs should hold your body in to the slope. Swing the club to the ball with the top of your body.

5 Because your legs are working to hold your body on the slope, the hip movement through will be at a minimum causing a restricted follow-through.

BALL PLUGGED IN GREENSIDE BUNKER

1 Note how the clubface has been turned in to a closed position and at the same time the grip is correct. Your stance should be square, with the ball positioned centrally between your feet. Feet set firmly in the sand.

4 Work with your legs and hips keeping your arms down in a position ready to hit a lot of sand.

2 Look at the sand several inches behind the ball. Set off on a smooth full swing.

5 Lots of sand will be hit to get the clubhead down and under the ball. The weight of the sand will open the clubhead. This is why you set the clubface closed.

3 At the top of backswing make a good shoulder turn. The clubface has kept its closed position.

6 Make every effort to follow through, but this is often hard. On these occasions getting the ball out of the bunker is about the best that you can hope for.

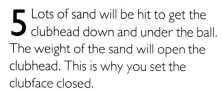

BALL IN A FAIRWAY BUNKER

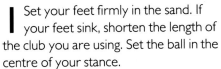

1 Set your feet firmly in the sand. If your feet sink, shorten the length of the club you are using. Set the ball in the centre of your stance.

2 As you take the clubhead up and away from the ball, look at the top of the ball and firm up your hold on the club. These points will help you take the ball more cleanly from the sand.

3 The firm hold on the club will restrict your wrist action. Take the club back with your body.

4 Full backswing, good shoulder turn and the club pointing parallel to the target as your body is set square to the ball-to-target line.

5 Your body-weight should be on your left side. Hands and arms ready to take the ball before you hit the sand.

6 Hold your head steady, take the ball quite cleanly off the sand. Your hands and arms release the club with your arms together as they were at address.

7 A well-balanced follow-through and the arms are now folded.

3 At impact you will first strike the ball, then a little sand. Swing the club past the body.

FAIRWAY BUNKER: EXAMPLE TWO

1 Embed your feet slightly into the sand to give a firm stance.

2 Your body and arms should be working together as you complete the backswing.

4 High follow-through, with your body facing the target.

Key Points Card

Points	Remarks
1	*Choose the club that will give you enough loft to get over the lip of the bunker*
2	*Keep a firm hold on the club.*
3	*Look at the top of the ball.*
4	*Make a smooth, balanced swing.*

THE PROFESSIONALS

Sergio Garcia of Spain playing from a greenside bunker. Here you can clearly see that the loft on the clubface has thrown the ball up and clear from the bunker.

BALL ON AN UPHILL LIE

Do not be ambitious on sloping lies. The uphill lie is probably the least difficult but it is essential that you are well-balanced and that you work with the slopes rather than fighting them. The main thing you have to work out when playing on an uphill lie is how to make the clubhead swing down and up the slope. To do this you have to set your body at right angles to the hill. This will make the golf club more lofted, so select a less lofted club to start off with. Note the action you are going to make will tend to hook the ball, so aim right of your intended target.

1 In setting the angle of your spine at right angles to the slope bend your left leg slightly more than usual.

2 This will restrict the movement of your hips through impact and is likely to make your hands more active and inclined to cross over.

Key Points Card

Points	Remarks
1	*The club you select will depend on the severity of the slope and how you have to stand to control your balance.*
2	*Remember that both hands work together.*
3	*Hold the grip firmly with the last three fingers of the right hand.*
4	*Play the ball off your left (the higher) leg.*

3 Play the ball off your higher leg, that is your left leg; this will help in setting your spinal angle and will give you room to swing the clubhead down and up the slope.

4 The angle that the body was set to the slope at the address has been maintained.

BALL ON A DOWNHILL LIE

The downhill lie is probably the most difficult of all the hazardous shots that you will have to play. When playing all awkward lies you must always play within your limits and not be too ambitious. First work out where you want the ball to come to rest. In the set-up stand so that it is possible to swing the club up and down the slope. You have to position the ball back from the centre of your stance and incline your body down the slope to make your spine vertical to the angle of the ball. Doing this will cancel the angle of loft on the clubface so it is important that you take a more lofted club than normal. Club selection will depend on the severity of the slope.

I Position the ball back from the centre of the stance.

2 You will now be bent into the slope and it will be difficult to make a complete body turn. Therefore, this is a hand and arm shot. The backswing will not be as complete as normal.

3 To take the ball cleanly off the ground keep the club low to the ground as it goes through impact.

4 Make every effort to keep your hands ahead of the clubhead when striking the ball. This will ensure the leading edge is square and that the clubhead moves down the slope.

5 Make a shortened follow-through and the ball should fly away low and straight.

BALL BELOW YOUR FEET

When the ball is below your feet the tendency is for the body to fall forward causing the backswing to go back on an upright plane and the hands to roll the clubface open. Consequently, you are likely to cut across the ball with an open face, sending the golf ball off swerving from left to right. As you will see from the following pictures the best way to play this shot will result in the ball flying high and only a short distance. You must accept this, rather than trying to gain extra distance through playing a more ambitious shot.

1 In the address position ensure that you use the full length of the golf club. Hold the grip near the end of the shaft.

2 Set the golf ball forward in your stance. Aim left of your target. Put more weight on your heels to avoid falling down the slope.

3 On the takeaway do not fight the slope. Use less body movement, and swing with your hands and arms.

4 Keep your balance as you hit the shot, let the club come down to impact with an open face.

5 Do not try and close it – this will result in you falling down the slope and fluffing the shot. Your follow-through will be restricted.

BALL ABOVE YOUR FEET

When the ball is above your feet the tendency is for the ball to hook. This is due to the fact that when you place the club to the ball the clubface will be facing to the left of your target. Also with the ball above your feet your swing plane becomes flatter.

1 Aim to the right of your intended target.

2 Hold the grip of the club several inches down from the top. If you use the full length of the club you risk hitting the ground before the ball. Set your body-weight into the slope to prevent falling backwards when you swing the club back and through.

3 The swing must be a smooth body and arm movement, without a lot of hand action.

4 This shows how the arm-swing has been flattened by the lie of the ball above the feet.

5 At impact, because of the danger of the slope, play with a lot of hand action. But note this closes the face of the club severely causing the shot to be smothered.

6 Well-balanced, with a flat follow-through showing how the club and swing accommodate the slope.

Key Points Card		
Points		*Remarks*
1		*Play with the ball in the middle of your stance.*
2		*Hold down the grip several inches.*
3		*Aim slightly right of the target to allow for the hook.*
4		*Set your balance into the slope.*
5		*The angle of the slope will cause a flatter swing plane and path. Do not resist this.*
6		*Keep the swing smooth.*

HIGH SHOTS OVER TREES

You may find yourself in the unfortunate position of having to play this rather awkward shot. In cases such as these it often pays not to be too ambitious and to work on getting the ball back into a playing position. In this case the ball has missed the fairway to the left and there are some large trees in the way. Club selection is of great importance. You will need some distance but the most important consideration is to have enough height to clear the trees. Each time you play an awkward shot like this, take time to imagine the flight line you require.

1 Set the ball forward in your stance, make sure your grip pressure is not too tight and think hard about the shot you are going to make.

2 At impact your shoulders should be very square helping to keep the loft on the clubface and your head well back to give an upward strike on the ball. Here the ball can be seen setting off in an upward lift.

3 See how the whole movement suggests the ball is being hit forward and up into the air. The ball has been taken cleanly off the ground.

4 Remain well-balanced, holding your body under the shot, turn your head and look underneath the ball.

Low Shots in Bushes

I If you need to restrict the uplift of the club on the backswing separate your hands from one another. Exactly how far apart you place them will depend on how far back you can take the club. You may need to bend your body low to get under the branches. Position the ball back in the stance which will make impact earlier.

DIFFICULT SHOTS

When the ball has to be lofted quickly, for example over a mound or out of a deep bunker, set the clubface open.

When you follow through playing from a greenside bunker or any high shot, hit through the ball and keep the loft on the club.

2 See here how the arms take the club back and the body-weight remains still. All these points help to avoid hitting the branches.

3 Impact is made with the right hand and arms, and the head is kept very still. The ball is now out and on to the fairway for the next shot.

LOW SHOTS UNDER TREES

1 Position the ball slightly back in the stance but make sure the left hand is still in line with the inside of your left leg. The head of the club will be slightly hooded if the leading edge is square to the target line. Flex your right leg inwards at the knee, which will settle your weight slightly on to your left side.

2 Swing the club back and up with your arms and hands. The legs and hips make very little movement and, therefore, your weight should not move to the right.

3 Keep your head still as your arms and legs pull the club down to the ball. Your hips should be square to the target line and your shoulders still back.

4 Keep your body low and punch the ball away with your forearms. Notice the left wrist position, this helps to take the loft off the club and keep the ball low.

EXAMPLE TWO

1 This shows the same shot but from behind the ball. From this position you can see how the ball must fly low.

2 The shoulders move to help the arms take the club back and the legs are flexed keeping a solid base to the swing.

3 The hands maintain a firm hold of the club, arms working closely together.

THE PROFESSIONALS

Tiger Woods has developed his upper body strength to ensure that when the time comes he can escape from a difficult lie. Here he uses his strength to punch the ball out of the rough.

4 The right shoulder moves down and through.

Key Points Card

Points	Remarks
1	Ball back slightly in the address.
2	Keep the leading edge of the club square, deloft (hood) the club.
3	As you strike the ball keep your hands and arms ahead of the club.
4	Keep your head still.

FAULTS AND PROBLEM SOLVING

If a golf ball is hit correctly it will fly straight towards the target. Shots that deviate to the left or right have been wrongly struck. The faults can be many and may be in your aim, your grip, your stance and your swing. In this chapter the pictures with pink shirts show errors being made and pictures with white shirts show the correct action.

Right, Luke Donald

SLICING

The slice is a ball that swings from left to right in its flight. As you will see from the pictures below the slice is caused by an open address position. This leads to an out-to-in swing path and the clubface being open to this swing path. The ball starts off flying on the swing path – to the left – but the open clubface puts spin on the ball and so it swerves round to the right. It is the swing path that directs the ball and the shape of the clubface at impact that spins the ball.

In the following pictures the clubs on the ground indicate parallel lines to the centre of the fairway, highlighting the open stance. In most cases players are not aware that they are making this error and they will still make an effort in the swing to send the clubface and ball to the fairway.

Always aim correctly for every shot. When you start with problems at the address the chances of making the correct back and through swing are made more difficult.

FRONT VIEW

1 Open set-up. The ball is a long way forward in the stance and the head is over the ball. Because of the open set-up the 'V's on both hands are pointing to the left shoulder which will cause an opening of the clubface during the swing.

2 The forward position of the ball and the open shoulders have restricted the shoulder turn. The club is now pointing left with the face open.

3 At impact the body is open. The hands are forward and the club is open to the body.

4 The club is travelling on the inside. The head is well forward, but there has been no release of the clubhead.

5 The follow-through is well left of the fairway and the clubhead is being held open by the hands.

SLICING: EXAMPLE TWO

1 This gives a clear view of a very open stance and alignment. The clubs on the ground indicate parallel lines to the centre of the fairway. In most cases the golfer is not aware he is making this error which leads to attempts to compensate in the swing in order to hit the ball straight.

2 Because of the open address, the arms have swung the club to the left of the target. In doing this the club was taken back on the outside and is now all set to swing down on the outside.

3 At impact, the shoulders and hips turn to the left of the target taking the arms inside the ball-to-target line. In attempting to hit the ball to the target the hands have now turned the clubface open to the swing path.

4 The clubhead moves through impact onto the inside path. The clubface is open. Therefore, the ball will start flying left because this is the direction of the swing path, but the open clubface puts spin on the ball, so it will swerve to the right once it is in its flight.

5 The head and shoulders are now well forward. The hands have not released the clubhead. The body is facing well left of the fairway.

PULLING

A pull is a shot that sends the ball flying straight to the left. It has the same swing path as the slice – out-to-in – but a different shaped clubhead at impact. The clubface is square at impact.

1 Notice how the set-up is the same as the set-up for the slice.

2 The swing is along the line of the body. As far as the target is concerned this golf club is 'laid off' – pointing to the left of the target. On the downswing the club will travel on the outside.

3 In the downswing you can see the club is about to travel down on the outside.

4 After impact the club is well over to the left, covering the ground called the inside. The ball is going to the left but stays straight because at impact the hands squared the clubface to this out-to-in swing path.

5 The follow-through shows that the clubhead was released along the out-to-in swing path.

HOOKING

A hook is the opposite shot to the slice, it sends the ball from right to left. The swing path is in-to-out, so the ball starts to the right following the swing path, but because the clubhead is closed at impact the ball spins round to the left. The hook is caused by errors in the set-up which in turn affect the swing plane and swing path.

I Here the whole alignment is facing well to the right of the centre of the fairway, showing a closed stance. This is opposite to the slice. On the takeaway the club will travel on the inside.

2 At the top of the backswing the club is pointing along the closed shoulder line, to the right of the target. This is known as being 'across the line'. The clubhead is closing; the clubface is facing the sky.

3 The downswing comes in very much on the inside, keeping the right side well back.

4 The club is moving on a swing path to the outside. The ball starts going to the right but because the hands turned the clubhead over, in an attempt to hit the ball to the target, the ball will spin off to the left.

5 The body is in the way so the arms are struggling to make a proper follow-through.

FLIGHT PATHS

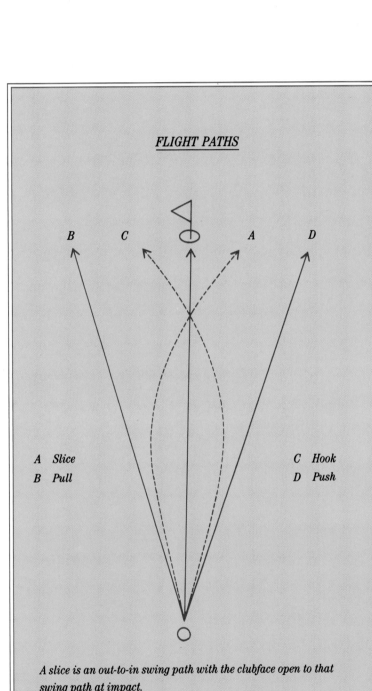

A   Slice
B   Pull

C   Hook
D   Push

A slice is an out-to-in swing path with the clubface open to that swing path at impact.

A pull is an out-to-in swing path with the clubface square to that swing path at impact.

A hook is an in-to-out swing path with the clubface closed to that swing path at impact.

A push is an in-to-out swing path with the clubface square to the target at impact.

FRONT VIEW

1 The ball is set back in the address. The feet, knees, hips and shoulders are aiming to the right of the target. Therefore, both 'V's are pointing more to the right shoulder.

2 As the club reaches the top of the backswing, notice the closed clubface and how the club points across the line of the club on the ground.

THE PROFESSIONALS

Severiano Ballesteros of Spain recovering from a hook into rough grass. With his swashbuckling style Ballesteros is a master at dealing with awkward lies and bunkers.

3 The ball is hit from the inside. The right shoulder is well back and not helping the club to move through impact.

4 The hands have turned the face over causing the hook. The ball will swerve to the left.

5 The fact that the right side was not helping the club through at impact shows now in the follow-through.

PUSHING

A push is the opposite shot to the pull, it sends the ball flying straight to the right. It has the same swing path as the hook – in-to-out – so the ball starts to the right, but because the clubhead is square to the swing path at impact the ball does not have spin on it, and stays straight in its flight path.

1 Once again the alignment is facing well to the right of the centre of the fairway. This is a closed stance.

2 At the top of backswing the club is pointing across the line and the clubface is closed.

3 This results in the attack on the ball being too much from the inside.

4 Impact is in-to-out and the clubface is square to the swing path. The ball starts right and flies straight along this line. Because the clubface was square at impact there is no side spin on the ball.

5 The ball was hit straight down the right side of the course.

PUSHING: EXAMPLE TWO

1 The set-up is facing to the right of target. The ball is well back in the stance, so the takeaway will go back quickly on the inside. This shot could be either a hook or a push.

2 The club closes at the top of the backswing. The shot could still be a hook or a push.

3 The swing path is on the inside and the clubface is square to this path. The shot is a push. The ball will fly straight to the right.

4 Because of the in-to-out swing path, the body is in the way of the follow-through and cannot clear.

TOPPING

This is the type of mistake that you are inclined to make when you are starting to play golf and have not learned to trust your movements. In the following examples note how the upward action has been made either with the body or the clubhead. This is incorrect as it is the loft on the face of the club that sends the ball in the air. In each case the position of the legs at the address, and how they work to turn the body and aid weight transference throughout the shot, need to be improved.

1 At the address the set-up is square and the posture is good. Everything looks ready for the backswing.

2 The club was swung to a good position by the hands and arms, but as you can see the legs have straightened causing the angle of the posture to rise. If the angle of the spine is not reset at this stage the club will hit the top half of the ball.

3 Just before impact. Sadly the legs and back have not recovered the angles that were set at the address. The hands and arms are trying to find the ball, but it is now too late, the top is imminent.

4 Everything except the ball is going up.

TOPPING: EXAMPLE TWO

1 The feet are a little closed and shoulders just a touch open. The head position is not set for a good shoulder pivot.

2 The head has to move to the right to allow for the shoulder turn. This causes the body to sway to the right as the arms and hands go back and up.

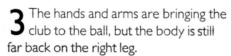

3 The hands and arms are bringing the club to the ball, but the body is still far back on the right leg.

4 This results in the ball being topped. Because of the sway back, the right side never helped the down and through swing to the moment of impact. The club was rising up on the ball at impact.

TOPPING: EXAMPLE THREE

1 All is set for the ball to be smashed straight down the middle, but the legs are possibly a little straight.

2 By now the legs are rather bent causing a loss of height, but a top could still be avoided. It might be possible to recover the position back to how it was at the address.

3 As the club is coming down to the impact area the body is moving up again, but there is still a chance of striking the ball in the correct place.

4 But the legs have straightened again, causing the top.

FLUFFING

The fluff is a shot where the club hits the ground before it hits the ball. It can occur with any type of shot at any time. As with topping, the problems often arise because of an incorrect position at the address. Always remember to check your alignment, stance and posture before you start the takeaway.

1 The address is looking good except that the golf ball is too far back in the stance. This may mean that the body-weight is incorrectly distributed at the start of the swing.

2 At the top of the backswing you can see that the hands and arms have taken the club back in a very upright manner. There has been little to no weight transferred to the right side.

3 On the downswing you can see the result of the ball being too far back in the stance combined with the upright arm movement on the backswing. The head is now too far forward, leaving no room to get a clean strike at the ball.

4 The arms did their best to get the clubhead to the ball but because of the steepness of the angle of attack the clubhead hit the ground.

FLUFFING: EXAMPLE TWO

1 The stance is a little closed which means the ball will be too far back.

2 The club has been swung back outside the ball-to-target line, therefore creating an upright position at the top of the backswing.

3 The address position and backswing make it difficult to take the ball cleanly off the tee. This picture shows clearly how the bottom of the swing arrived too early, hence the amount of ground being moved.

4 This results in a restricted follow-through. Due to the upright arm-swing in the takeaway only the arms create the follow-through.

FLUFFING: EXAMPLE THREE

1 Once again you can see the address with the wood. The ball is teed-up correctly, but the shoulders are set slightly open to the feet and hips.

2 Because the top half of the body has lifted the club up to the top of the backswing, the right leg is very straight and the angle of the spine has been altered from the address.

3 On the downswing, the legs and body make a great effort to return to the level set at the address so that the ball can be taken off the tee.

4 Even though the recovery effort went on right into impact, the body continued to go down and the club could only hit the ground in front of the ball.

OVER-SWINGING

The over-swing is a common error. Whilst you notice it mainly at the top of the backswing, the next set of pictures demonstrate that the faults can actually be seen right at the beginning of the swing. First, look at the incorrect swings. Then compare them to the correct swing.

ARM-SWING AND BODY TURN AT THE START OF THE SWING

I The club is well on its way to the backswing. It has clearly been taken back with virtually no help from the body. The clubhead has moved much more than any other part. As a result the left arm has started to bend at the elbow. The club was taken back too far, too fast, too soon.

2 At the top of the backswing, in spite of making some movement the body has not caught up with the club. Now, the left arm is a little more bent, the arms are further apart, and the head and shaft of the club have gone beyond the horizontal line.

3 You can see clearly how the arms separated at the top of the backswing. At this stage recovery can still be made but it will be difficult to produce a consistent shot.

4 Notice the splayed formation of the arms on the follow-through which suggests that the complete recovery was not made.

ERROR: EXAMPLE TWO

1 The ball and clubhead were set on the ball-to-target line at the address, with the feet, hips and shoulders parallel to this line. The body is making a good pivoting movement, but the arms and club have come up to join the body. Because of this the club moved slightly inside the ball-to-target line.

2 This shows the same action but from the front. Despite the good body movements the arms have brought the club up flat to the body losing the alignment to the target.

ERROR: EXAMPLE THREE

1 Again the clubhead and ball were set square to the target at the address. But only the arms have taken the club up, and in so doing it has gone slightly on the outside of the ball-to-target line. With this arm-swing, the body is moving along the ball-to-target line instead of pivoting.

2 This shows the same action but from the front. The body has moved sideways and the head and shoulders are down. This is an arm-swing without the correct body turn.

THE CORRECT SWING

The first picture shows the start of the backswing from an address position that was square to the ball-to-target line. The clubhead and shaft have been taken to about waist height with a turning movement of the left shoulder, left hip and a swinging movement of the left arm and the whole of the club. The right shoulder, right arm and right hip have in no way stopped the left side making this movement. The head position is held steady, the pressure of the hands on the club maintained, the right leg is still flexed as it was in the address.

Take note that the hands and the face of the club have worked together without any independent wrist movement, also that the left arm and the club are now parallel to the ball-to-target line. This one-piece movement has brought the club slightly on the inside of the target line.

If at this stage you were to look at your hold on the grip you would see that the 'V'-shapes of your hands were still pointing between your face and right shoulder, as they were at the address.

This second picture shows the same position but from the front. Because the club and the left side have moved to the right some weight has been transferred on to the instep of the right foot. The right leg has kept its position which will create the hip turn. The position of the head and spinal angle have been maintained, promoting the correct turn and tilt of the shoulders. The arms and club have remained the same distance apart as they were at the address.

Again you can see how the hands and clubface have moved together. Controlling the shape of the clubhead and its direction at the start of the backswing is of great importance. This is a one-piece takeaway.

Opposite: Fred Couples.

Errors in the Short Game

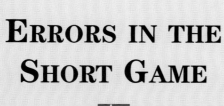

Although pitching, chipping and putting are all part of the short game, the elements of these shots are the same as for full shots – you want the ball to end up where you have aimed it. As such some errors are similar to those discussed in the previous chapter, but these shots also present their own problems, not least the problem of dealing with pressure. The pictures with pink shirts are the ones where errors are being shown and the white or blue shirts show the correct action.

Right, Phil Mickelson

ERRORS IN PITCHING

The pitch is a shot that is used to hit the ball straight and in the air. Therefore, you must first select a club with loft on it such as a 9-iron, wedge or sand wedge. These will give you the height on the shot that you need. As in all shots, for the pitch you start by lining up the leading edge of the club square to the target. It should be at right angles to the ball-to-target line.

Three types of errors are shown below. Firstly, topping, otherwise known as thinning. Secondly, fluffing, otherwise known as hitting the ball flat. This is when you hit the ground before you hit the ball. Thirdly, there is the socket. This dreadful shot is when you hit the ball with the heel of the club and is commonly known as a shank.

TOPPING

1 It is tempting to imagine that leaning back on the right leg, with the hands back, will lift the ball up and over the bunker. But this ignores the fact that it is the loft on the club that sends the ball into the air.

2 In this address position the club will be taken back with the hands and wrists holding on to the club, not letting the wrists cock. Also see how the head has moved to the left, perhaps with the idea that it should be kept down.

3 Contact is made with the leading edge of the club so the ball is hit into the bunker. See how all the effort seems to be going into lifting the ball up in the air. The head is to the right, the hands have stopped and the clubhead is up in the air, causing impact to be halfway up the side of the ball. The left heel is off the ground, which is helping to make a lifting action.

4 This detail shows the position of the club at impact. There is no loft on this part of the club. You should strike the ball in the centre of the clubface.

5 In the completed swing the body is well back, with the left foot more off the ground and the arms and hands still trying to lift the ball over the bunker.

FLUFFING

1 The miscalculation here is the belief that if you take a lofted club and hit down at the ball it will go into the air. This explains why the ball is so far back in the stance and the body-weight and head so far forward. In truth, standing like this will probably take loft off the clubface.

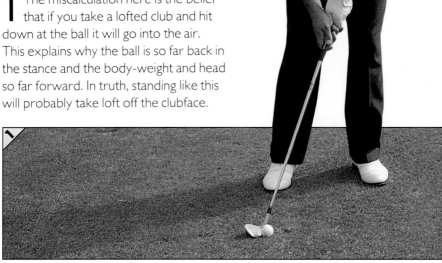

2 The club is taken up and back quite severely with the hands and arms. You can see more clearly here how far ahead of the ball the player is standing.

3 In the picture you can see very clearly that the ground has been hit before the ball. The ball is airborne but it will not make the distance required because it was hit too far up the clubface. This part of the club does not propel the ball forward with any speed.

4 Due to the steep angle of attack, the follow-through is very restricted. This is a good example of the loft on the clubface not being used correctly.

THE SOCKET

1 Notice how the hands and arms have taken the club back too far on the inside of the ball-to-target line.

2 The wrists are too cocked, taking the club too far back. If the clubhead is brought straight down from this position the swing path will be in-to-out, and the ball will fly to the right.

3 Here though, instead of swinging in-to-out, an attempt is made to correct the backswing. The shoulders have turned but at impact the clubhead is slightly further away from the body. The heel of the club, the socket, collides with the ball.

4 This picture illustrates the position of the clubhead at impact.

5 The body has come up because the club and arms swung out and around on the downswing, and at impact.

CORRECT PITCH

1 Comfortable address, clubhead and ball aiming at the target.

2 Hands and arms take the club straight back and up.

3 Impact, then the club and arms swing towards the flag.

4 The right side helps the movement to the target.

5 The weight is on the left side in a well-balanced follow-through.

ERRORS IN CHIPPING

The chip is a shot that can be played with the putter if the ground between the ball and the green is clean and fast. The chip must travel straight and on a low trajectory because it is a running shot. As in pitching, once you have selected the stroke you intend to play, you must not change your mind. Judging the distance on these shots can only come from plenty of practice. When chipping you must avoid opening and closing the clubhead during the swing. The stroke needs to be played without wrist action so that the clubhead can be kept close to the ground throughout the playing of the shot. It is very similar to the putt. The following pictures show a couple of common errors.

I The medium iron has been selected and the address position is looking good – slightly more weight on the left leg, clubface a little hooded to help the ball run, and hands down the grip to reduce the size of the backswing.

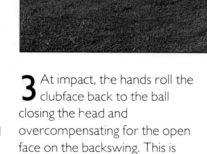

2 This is where the mistake occurs. There appears to have been a change of plan – the hands and wrists have taken the clubhead back into an open position. This is the action you would use if you intended to play a lofted shot.

3 At impact, the hands roll the clubface back to the ball closing the head and overcompensating for the open face on the backswing. This is seen clearly by the position of the right hand and the shape of the clubhead.

4 The clubhead continues in this rolling manner sending the ball too far and to the left.

2 On the backswing, note how the clubhead has not stayed low to the ground but has been picked up by the hands. The clubface now has too much loft on it for this shot.

ERROR: EXAMPLE TWO

1 The ball is lying well on the fairway, just short of the apron of the green. A medium iron has been chosen for this chip and run shot. At the address the hands are too far back and behind the ball, which will cause the clubhead to be more lofted than is necessary. Also the body-weight is incorrect. It should set slightly more on the left leg than the right.

3 Partly because the body-weight is too central only the right hand and arm have been used to bring the club to the impact area. See how the left hand, head and arm have stopped, causing the clubhead to rise when it strikes the ball and, therefore, topping it.

4 Further on through the shot, the clubhead is a long way from the ground. The left hand and arm stopped when the strike was made. On this occasion the ball will probably shoot right across the green, no doubt finishing in some trouble.

CORRECT CHIP

Remember when you want a low shot, keep the clubhead low to the ground on both the back and the through swing, making every effort to ensure that the arms and club move as far forward through the shot as they moved back on the backswing.

1 Hands down the grip; leading edge square; well-balanced address.

2 Just before impact the body is still and the left hand and shaft together. Clubhead delofted.

3 At impact the arms and club return together to the ball. The clubhead is low to the ground.

4 Now the ball is on its way, flying low. The club, hands and arms have moved together, and in so doing, have kept the clubhead low to the ground.

5 The body is well-balanced; the ball is about to land and then roll up to the target, the flag.

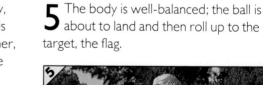

ERRORS IN PUTTING

If you are to make the ball roll into the hole on the putting green successfully then you must make sure that the ball starts along the correct line. The following pictures illustrate some of the common errors which cause disappointment on the green. Remember that you must align the ball with the centre of the clubhead, and set the ball in a position that enables you to take the putter back smoothly, low to the ground. The fewer movements you make with your hands and wrists when taking the clubhead backwards and forwards, the better.

The ball is lined up with the toe of the putter. This may cause the ball to roll to the right, and very often short, of the hole.

2 The golf ball is in line with the heel of the putter. This will hit the ball left of the target. From this point on the club it is also hard to make the ball roll smoothly.

Here the body is set square to the hole, but the head is not over the line of the putt. The hands are also a little low, with the ball too far away.

2 The hands and arms have taken the putter back from the ball, outside the ball-to-hole line. A good putting action would have taken the putter back along the ball-to-hole line. On a longer putt it would have gone slightly on the inside.

3 Just before impact, you can see the putter head on the line of the target. The ball will be struck with the heel of the putter.

4 The putter head is well to the left of the hole, the hands have tried to square up the clubface. This action is responsible for a lot of missed putts from all lengths.

ERROR: EXAMPLE TWO

1 The set-up appears to be aiming to the right of the hole, with the golf ball displaced towards the toe of the putter. The tendency from here is to swing the putter head back too much on the inside of the line.

2 As the putter head is just about to make contact, see how the putter face is now aiming very much to the right, so the clubface is open to the hole. As this is a level putt and there is no need to allow for any slope on the green there is not much chance of the ball rolling towards the hole.

3 The ball is away. You can see clearly that the swing of the putter head back and through was in no way able to send the ball to the hole.

4 The ball continues to move away from the hole.

2 The result of this address position is that the action at the start of the stroke is made by the wrists. They almost pick the putter head up.

ERROR: EXAMPLE THREE

1 The golf ball is a long way back in the stance. Therefore, the face of the putter cannot be at right angles to the ground and the leading edge of the putter will be tilted sharply into the putting surface.

THE PROFESSIONALS

Bernhard Langer of Germany having missed a putt at Kiawah, South Carolina, during the 1991 Ryder Cup. This tragedy at the final hole cost the European team the trophy.

3 The putter head comes down to the ball with the action being made by the hands and wrists.

4 The putter head will then hit the ground as it strikes the ball and come to a stop.

ERROR: EXAMPLE FOUR

1 See here how the shaft of the putter comes straight up, the forearms splay out and the elbows are bent. Having set this angle for the shaft of the club and the arms, it must be kept the same if you are to make a smooth stroke.

2 But as the putter went back the hands went forward to the hole. This changes the way the arms are set compared to their position at the address. The shaft and the left arm are now in line with one another.

3 An effort has been made to take the left hand and arm back to their position in the address. Now the right arm and the putter are in line.

4 The whole action is loose and wristy causing very poor contact on the ball.

ERROR: EXAMPLE FIVE

1 Everything appears to be going well. The putter is going back low to the ground. Hands, arms and putter moving together, no wrist break.

2 The putter has reached the right point in the backswing for this length of putt. But what you cannot see on looking at this picture is that the golfer can see the hole out of the corner of his left eye.

3 The moment the ball was played the player started to look at the hole, causing the shoulders to turn and brake the forward momentum of the clubhead towards the hole.

4 Now he will have to will the ball to keep moving.

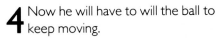

ERROR: EXAMPLE SIX

1&2 Again the error here is that the head has moved. Practise these short putts keeping your head still and listening for the ball to go into the hole.

3 Here you can see that the head is still with the shoulders square.

ERROR: EXAMPLE SEVEN

1–3 Here the head has kept still but far too much hand and wrist action has been used.

4 Here the hands, arms and putter are all working together.

RULES AND ETIQUETTE

With the increasing popularity of golf, courses are becoming more crowded and it is therefore all the more important that you are considerate to other players at all times. In this chapter the basic rules of the game and types of matches you might like to play are examined. But always check the local rules before you start to play.

TYPES OF MATCHES

MATCH-PLAY

Match-play is a hole by hole contest. The scores are worked out according to how many holes each player wins or loses. For example, if after 16 holes player A has won three holes more than player B he or she cannot lose. Player A would have won the match 3 & 2 (three holes up, and only two to play). The most any player can win by is 10 & 8. Should the match be all square after 18 holes this could be what is called a halved match, but if a result is required the players will move to the first hole and start again until someone wins a hole. If player A wins the first extra hole the result will read that he won at the 19th.

STROKE-PLAY (MEDAL-PLAY)

In stroke-play you count the total number of strokes for the round. One round is 18 holes.

STABLEFORD

This is a format of play where you score points. Points are awarded according to how many strokes under or over par that the player takes at each hole. The total number of points scored at each hole added together gives the score.

Par+2 (Double bogey)	0 pts
Par+1 (Bogey)	1 pt
Par	2 pts
Par−1 (Birdie)	3 pts
Par−2 (Eagle)	4 pts
Par−3 (Albatross)	5 pts

FOURSOME

Foursome is a partnership game in which players take alternate shots with the same ball. The golfer who plays from the first tee drives at all the odd numbered holes and their partner tees off on the even numbered holes. This game can be played as either match-play, stroke-play or stableford against two other players.

Opposite: Robertson and Old Tom Morris.

Nowhere in the world is golf becoming more popular than in Japan. Golfing ranges provide golfers who live in the city with a chance to practise.

153

FOUR BALL

Four ball is another partnership game. This time two players play the better of their two balls against the better ball of their opponents. This is a form of match-play. You can also have a four ball better ball stroke-play or stableford. The four ball method of play is perhaps the most popular, but its biggest drawback is that it can take rather a long time to complete a round.

THREE BALL AND THREESOME

The three ball is a match where each player plays against one another. The threesome is a match with one player playing their ball against two partners playing alternate shots with one ball.

THE SCORE CARD

Each player is responsible for their own score card even though the score is kept by the other players. There is a space on the card for each player to record their own score as a marker. Never sign your own card if the score is incorrect. Always see that the correct handicap is shown on the card and the number of strokes received. Each player should check their hole by hole score and their gross and nett total.

Marker's Score	Hole	Yards	Metres	Par	Stroke Index	Score A	Score B	Nett Score	Stableford Points
	1	426	390	4	11				
	2	353	323	4	3				
	3	407	372	4	7				
	4	202	185	3	15				
	5	341	312	4	13				
	6	488	446	5	1				
	7	150	137	3	17				
	8	414	379	4	9				
	9	413	378	4	5				
OUT		3194	2922	35					
	10	280	256	4	14				
	11	374	342	4	8				
	12	181	166	3	18				
	13	475	434	5	4				
	14	198	181	3	16				
	15	428	391	4	2				
	16	344	315	4	12				
	17	417	381	4	6				
	18	476	435	5	10				
IN		3173	2901	36					
OUT		3194	2922	35					
TOTAL		6367	5823	71					

COMPETITION
DATE
Player A   TIME   Handicaps   Strokes Rec'd
Player B   PAR 71   SSS 71

HANDICAP
NETT

Markers Signature ....

Players Signature ....

Please sign and return your card after each round of golf

Above, A scorecard from the Royal Birkdale Golf Club

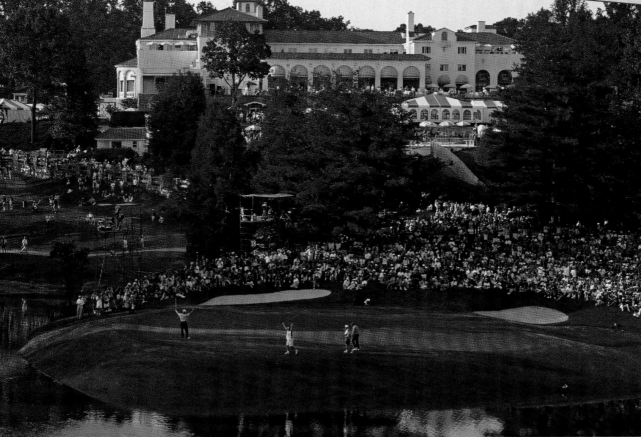

Left, The magnificent club house at Congressional Country Club, Bethesda, Maryland, USA.

THE PAR

The par of the course is made up by the yardage or meters of each hole.

Yards	Metres	Par
0 – 250	0 – 229	3
251 – 475	230 – 434	4
476 +	435 +	5

STROKE INDEX

The playing difficulty of each hole, as assessed by the club, is taken into account and a stroke index is allocated to each hole (see under handicap for further details).

TEE POSITIONS

Where possible each club will have the following tee positions permanently marked and measured: Ladies Medal Tees - Red; Mens Forward Tees – Yellow; Mens Medal Tees – White.

Below, Vijay Singh during the play-off for the USPGA 2004 at Whistling Straits, Wisconsin, USA.

HANDICAPS

Handicapping is a system whereby strokes are subtracted from the scores of weaker players to enable golfers of different standards to compete fairly against one another. Handicaps are issued by golf clubs and authorized amateur golf associations.

HANDICAP ALLOWANCES

MATCH-PLAY
In match-play the handicap allowance is worked out as ¾ of the difference between the players handicaps. For example, if player A is a 25 handicap and player B is a 10 handicap, the difference is 15. Three-quarters of 15 is 11¼, therefore, player A receives 11 strokes. These are taken at the holes where the figure 11 and under appears on the stroke index on the score card. If the difference does not come out to a whole number it is rounded up.

STROKE-PLAY (MEDAL-PLAY)
In stroke-play you must complete every hole, then the whole handicap is deducted from the total score of the 18 holes completed. If the total score is 90, less a handicap of 15, the score is 75.

SINGLE STABLEFORD
The allowance for single stableford is ⅞ths of the total handicap. For example, if the player has a handicap of 19, ⅞ths of 19 is 16.625, this is rounded up to 17. These strokes are taken at the holes where 17 and below are shown on the stroke index.

FOUR BALL MATCH-PLAY
Each player receives ¾ of the difference in handicap taken from the lowest handicap of the four players. The strokes are taken at the holes indicated on the stroke index.

FOURSOME MATCH-PLAY
In foursome match-play, add together the handicap of each partnership.

FOURSOME STABLEFORD
Each pairing receives ⅞₁₆ of their combined handicap; these strokes are taken at the holes indicated on the stroke index.

FOURSOME STROKE-PLAY
Each pairing receives ½ of their combined handicap, this is then taken from their gross score for the completed 18 holes.

Fred Couples and his caddy approaching the green at the Masters, 1992. Caddies are amongst other things responsible for the care of the equipment and measuring distances. Some players build up a strong relationship with their caddy, keeping the same one for years.

FOURSOME STABLEFORD BETTER-BALL

Each player receives ⅞ths of their handicap. These strokes are taken at the holes indicated on the stroke index. The better ball of the two players is the score for each hole. Total points recorded is the team score.

FOUR BALL BETTER-BALL STROKE-PLAY

Each player receives ¾ of their handicap. Each pair then records their best gross and nett score for each hole, using the stroke index, the best nett score on each hole will be the pairings score.

Golf is a game of world-wide popularity. This is the 18th green and clubhouse at Monastir, Tunisia.

RULES

There are a universal set of rules for golf that are constantly reviewed in Scotland by the Royal and Ancient Golf Club of St Andrews and in America by the United States Golf Association. Outlined below are some of the most important rules, but always check to see if a club has any special local rules of its own.

A modern set of irons.

STARTING OUT

Before play commences announce to your opponent the number and make of the ball you are going to start with.

You are only permitted to have fourteen clubs in your bag. They do not have to be different clubs, you can have two putters, several different wedges and sand wedges. It is the maximum number of fourteen that is important. Penalties are incurred for carrying more clubs and they are given regardless of the number of extra clubs. For stroke-play two penalty strokes are given on each hole on which the violation occurred, with a maximum penalty of four strokes. In match-play you lose the hole on which the violation occurred, with a maximum penalty per round of the loss of two holes. When playing stableford deduct two points from the final tally for each hole on which a violation occurred, maximum deduction four points.

THE HONOUR
Who is going to hit the ball first? This is called the honour. If it is an organized competition the honour is taken by the player whose name appears first for that game. Otherwise decide by tossing a coin.

THE TEEING GROUND
This is a flat prepared area, which will have two tee markers on it. These are usually stuck in the ground and can easily be moved by the ground staff to a different part of the tee to save wear on any one place. The tee of the day is a rectangle extending back two club lengths from a line between the markers. The ball must be teed-up within this area although you may stand outside it if you wish.

In match-play if you tee-up from outside the teeing ground your opponent can recall the shot played and ask you to take it again.

There is no penalty. In stroke-play you are penalized by two strokes and must then play from within the teeing ground. Strokes played from outside the teeing ground do not count. If you fail to return to the tee before you tee-off on the next hole, or leave the 18th green you are disqualified.

BALL FALLING OFF THE TEE PEG

This happens quite frequently. Even if the ball is teed-up in the correct way it may fall off of the tee at the address, or you might touch it with the clubhead and knock it off the tee. There is no penalty for this. Replace the ball on the tee peg and play away. However, if you have started your downswing when the ball topples from the tee and you are unable to check before impact, making a glancing blow on the ball or even missing it, this counts as a stroke. You cannot replace the ball on the tee peg. Should you be able to stop your downswing this does not constitute a stroke.

BALL IN PLAY

Once the game has begun the ball must be played as it lies, which means that you cannot touch it or improve its lie during the play to the green. Some courses do have a local rule which permits you to move the ball. This is often the case during the winter when the preferred lie rule can be introduced. The preferred lie rule entitles you to pick up the ball and replace it within 6 in (152 mm) of its original position, but it cannot be placed closer to the hole. If the ball comes to rest in casual water, it has to be dropped in accordance with the rules.

During the playing of each hole you are not permitted to play any practice strokes. A stroke is defined as the forward movement of the club with the intention of striking the ball. It is quite in order to have practice swings, but when doing this do not cause damage to the turf, also do not hold up play.

Pressing down the ground behind the ball, improving its lie, is not allowed at anytime once the ball is in play.

Below: Leaves and twigs being moved from around the ball. This is quite in order as long as you do not move the ball, but the items that are moved must be dead. You cannot break off any vegetation that is growing.

PLAYING THE WRONG BALL

Always make sure the ball you are about to play is your own; should you play the wrong ball you incur penalties. In match-play, you lose the hole. In stroke-play, add a two-stroke penalty and then play your own ball. If the ball you played belongs to a fellow competitor it must be replaced. The penalties do not apply if you are playing in a hazard.

LOST BALL

If your ball is lost you are allowed five minutes to look for it. Whenever this happens always tell the match behind you to play through. In match- and stroke-play, if after five minutes you cannot find the ball go back to where you played your last shot. If it was on the tee, tee-up a new ball, and if it was on the fairway or in the rough drop a new ball as near as possible to the spot where you played your last stroke. Add a penalty shot and lose the distance the ball went, for example, if your ball is lost from the tee shot your next shot will be counted as your third. This is known as stroke and distance.

BALL UNFIT FOR PLAY

If the ball is visibly damaged, by a cut or a crack, or has gone out of shape so that its true flight or roll is affected you can replace it without penalty. Make sure you consult with your opponent or marker. This does not apply for mud stuck to the side of the ball or if the paint is scratched.

BALL OUT OF BOUNDS

As with the lost ball, you apply the stroke and distance rule. Go back to where you played your last shot and add a penalty shot. Check the score card for out of bounds areas. It is the club's duty to define its boundaries. You can stand out of bounds to hit a ball that is in bounds.

DROPPING THE BALL

Stand upright and hold the ball at shoulder height. Drop the ball. If the ball touches you before it hits the ground it must be redropped, and you do not incur a penalty. You can be facing in any direction when dropping the ball.

Hazards

Ground under Repair

This is an area where course maintenance is going on and will be clearly marked, often with a sign stating G.U.R. If your ball is in this area drop it clear at the nearest point of relief without penalty.

Casual Water

If water is visible as you take your stance when playing through the green you are entitled to a free drop. This must be taken at the nearest point which avoids these conditions. It may mean your ball is on the fairway but the nearest point is in the rough – bad luck. Having determined the nearest point of relief drop the ball within one club-length of that point.

Bunkers

A bunker is an area of bare ground most often a depression, which is usually covered in sand. The grass-covered banks of a bunker are not part of the bunker. Bunkers can be found anywhere on the golf course but mainly they are situated around the green.

When playing a stroke out of a bunker you must not ground the club in the sand when addressing the ball. Neither can you touch the sand on the backswing. Remember you cannot touch the sand in a bunker, or the ground in a hazard before you play a stroke. The penalty for this is two strokes in stroke play and loss of a hole in match-play. Always rake the bunker after you have played out to ensure the surface is smooth for the next unfortunate player to follow you there.

Opposite: When dropping the ball on the course, stand upright and hold the ball at shoulder height.

You must not ground the club into the sand when playing in a bunker.

WATER HAZARDS

It is the duty of the club to define clearly the limits of a water hazard, this is usually done by means of yellow stakes or lines marked on the ground. The water level at times may not extend to the stakes or lines set by the club committee, leaving dry or grassy banks between the stakes and the water. This defined area is still a water hazard. If you wish you can play your ball as it lies, but you cannot ground your club or touch the hazard during the address or backswing. The alternative is to drop your ball either under the stroke and distance rule, or for a penalty of one stroke you can drop the ball anywhere behind the hazard, keeping the point where your ball last crossed the line of the hazard between you and the hole.

When dropping the ball make sure you stand so that you are dropping the ball on this line, not to either side.

LATERAL WATER HAZARD

This hazard is water that lies more or less in the direction of the line of play. In most occasions this is a trench for drawing surface water from the fairways. Again the area of the hazard will be defined either with lines on the ground or red stakes.

In this case you can either drop the ball under the water hazard rules, or within two club lengths either side of the hazard, opposite where your ball went into the defined area, under a one-stroke penalty.

The Green

Having started the hole together on the tee, you finish the hole together on the green. It is here that pressure is at its greatest, therefore, good conduct is of great importance. Always look after the surface of the green particularly around the hole. Never take your trolley on to the green; park it at the point where you will exit to the next hole. Equally if you are carrying your bag of clubs, get into the habit of laying them down off the green. Always repair your own pitch marks.

Never walk on the line of another player's putt; if you are asked to attend the flag, stand

A water hazard at the 10th hole at the Belfry.

Opposite: Always repair your own pitch marks on the green.

well clear of the hole, holding the flag at arm's length, making sure the flag will come out easily before the player putts. When replacing the flag avoid marking the rim of the hole. You can mark your ball, lift it and clean it at anytime on the green. This is done by putting a coin or ball marker, into or on the surface behind the ball. If your ball is on the line of another player's putt you might be asked to mark it.

Once you are on the green ensure that you either have someone to attend to the flag or that you take it out of the hole. If you hit the flag when putting in match-play you lose one hole, and in stroke-play it counts as a two-stroke penalty. This rule applies even if the flag is out of the hole lying on the green, so be sure it is not in your line. In match-play if your ball is on the green and your ball strikes your opponent's ball, you lose one hole. In stroke-play you are penalized by two strokes and the balls are played as they lie.

A ball marker.

THE WORLD OF
CHAMPIONSHIP
GOLF

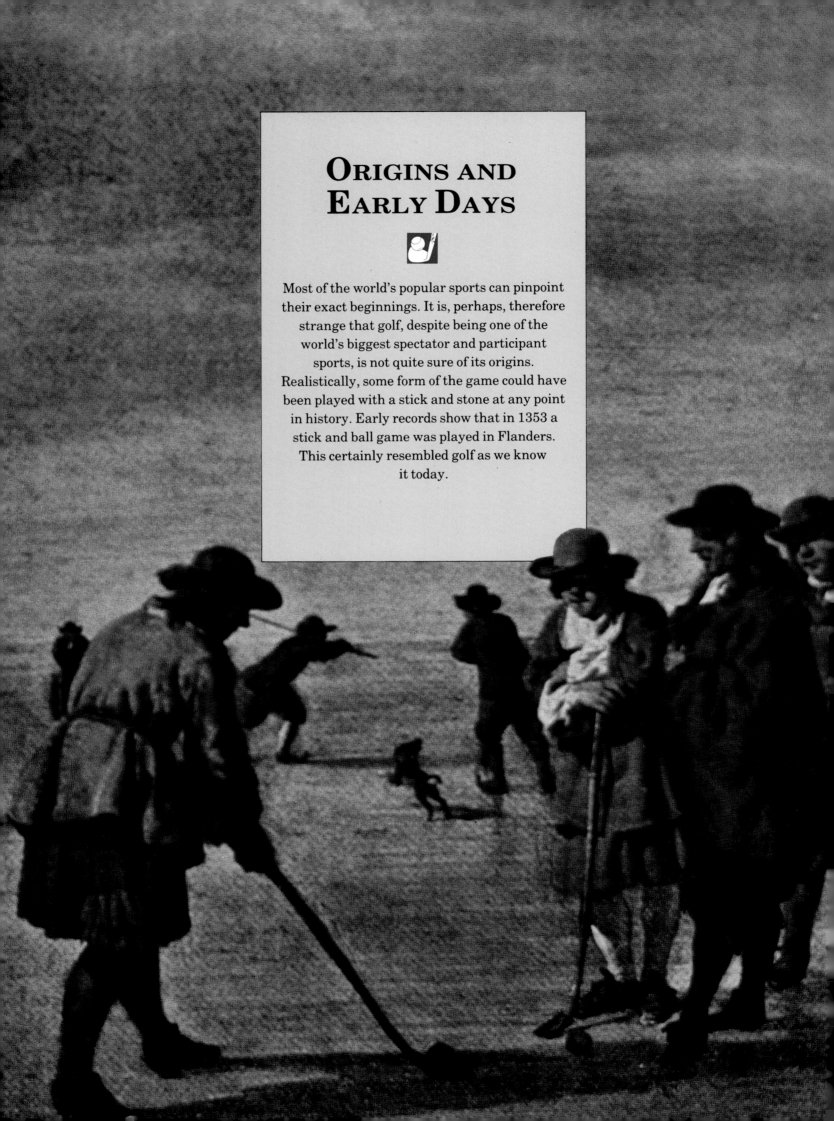

ORIGINS AND EARLY DAYS

Most of the world's popular sports can pinpoint their exact beginnings. It is, perhaps, therefore strange that golf, despite being one of the world's biggest spectator and participant sports, is not quite sure of its origins. Realistically, some form of the game could have been played with a stick and stone at any point in history. Early records show that in 1353 a stick and ball game was played in Flanders. This certainly resembled golf as we know it today.

The Dutch played a similar game to the Belgians, and they called it *kolf* which, if not the same as the modern game, certainly sounded like it. Around the same time a stained-glass window was commissioned for Gloucester Cathedral, England, by Sir Thomas Broadstone, depicting a man swinging a stick at a ball. This is the basis of an English claim to being the game's inventors. But the Scots would dispute this. They firmly believe they founded golf and, indeed, their claim is strong, because golf's heritage and lore has primarily evolved on the Scottish links.

It is certain that golf, as it is known today, was played in Scotland in the fifteenth century because golf was banned in 1457 by an Act of Parliament as it interfered with archery practice. There were three such edicts. The last was in 1491 by James IV but ten years later he himself took up the game and this is when it gained royal recognition.

Previous page: St. Andrews.

Opposite: Golf in Holland.

The so-called 'Gloucester golfer' window. This is the basis of the English claim to being the game's inventors.

Left: James IV of Scotland. In 1491 he issued the third edict banning golf.

Below: The Honourable Company of Edinburgh Golfers.

Around sixty years or so later, Mary Queen of Scots gave the game her royal approval and in the mid-sixteenth century the Archbishop of St Andrews gave his consent for the game to be played in the Burgh. Golf was now becoming a popular game in Scotland and its claim to be the 'home' of golf is not questioned, even if the game's actual origin still remains uncertain.

By the eighteenth century, the game had spread throughout Scotland and its participants were no longer confined to the ranks of royalty and nobility. In the middle of the century, organized clubs started to develop. The Edinburgh Golfing Society, later the Royal Burgess Golfing Society of Edinburgh, was formed in 1735 and it therefore has the distinction of being the world's oldest golf club.

In 1744 the Gentlemen Golfers of Edinburgh, later renamed the Honourable Company of Edinburgh Golfers, was formed at Leith and they were responsible for drawing up golf's first set of rules.

When the St Andrews Club (later renamed the Royal and Ancient) was formed in 1754, their rules were almost identical to those of the Edinburgh Golfers. But one thing that

was not the same was the length of their respective courses: the Leith links had five holes while St Andrews had 22 spread over their 11 huge greens. It was after the latter reduced theirs to 18 holes in 1764 that other courses followed suit, and 18 became the standard number of holes for subsequent courses.

The growth of golf in Scotland led, inevitably, to the game being taken south 'over the border' to England and, while the game had been played by the Prince of Wales at Greenwich as early as 1608, the first English club dates from 1766 with the formation of the Royal Blackheath Club. Perhaps surprisingly, the game bypassed mainland Europe and one of the first clubs outside Britain was set up by expatriates

Calcutta, in 1829. Originally known as the Calcutta Club, it later became the Royal Calcutta Club.

The first club on continental Europe was founded at Pau in France in 1856 and by the end of the nineteenth century golf had spread to many more parts of the globe; and Australia, New Zealand and Canada were all swept up in one of the world's greatest games. Inevitably the United States would soon fall under the spell of this fast-growing sport, but it took a while for it to catch on there. In fact early attempts to develop the game in America had failed after the Crail Golfing Society, South Carolina, was wound up shortly after its formation in 1786. It was to be nearly one hundred years before the next serious attempt to form a club in the

USA, but that, too, was short-lived and the Oakhurst Club in Virginia also failed. But when the St Andrews Club in Yonkers, New York, was formed in 1888 with many British members, it helped popularize the game in America. By 1894 the United States Golf Association was formed, and the greatest golf-playing nation in the world burst into life.

Organized clubs led to organized competitions, and many of the earliest matches in Scotland and England were four-ball money matches. In 1860 a competition was organized in Britain to find the champion golfer, following the death a year earlier of the 'uncrowned' champion, Allan Robertson. And so was born the British Open, which was played over three rounds of Prestwick's 12-hole course and won by Willie Park with a score over 36 holes of 174.

Golf at Prestwick, Scotland by Michael Brown. The first British Open was played here.

The United States hosted its first Open in 1895 at Newport, Rhode Island, where the first winner was Horace Rawlins. Since then major championships, for professionals and amateurs, have developed all over the world and, of course, such has been the rivalry between golfing nations that team tournaments, such as the Walker Cup and the Ryder Cup, have also been established.

Opposite: Golf at Pau in France, by Allen Sealy, 1892.

Below left: A painting of Victorian ladies playing golf.

Below right: Golf being played on the Scheldt, c.1600.

EVOLUTION AND EQUIPMENT

Golf has come a long way since its beginnings 500 or more years ago. Today it is a multi-million dollar business, for players, sponsors, television companies and, of course, golf equipment manufacturers.

With the constant drive to develop clubs that will hit harder and balls that will fly further, one has to wonder just how the golfing greats of yesteryear, such as Robertson, Old and Young Tom Morris, and Harry Vardon, would have fared with the modern technology that has produced so much 'game improving' equipment.

THE GOLF BALL

Manufacturers are constantly seeking ways of aiding the golfer in his quest to hit the ball from tee to green via the quickest and most

A 'feathery' golf ball, c. 1845. The 'feathery' was a cased leather ball stuffed with feathers. Being hand-made it was not fully rounded and lacked uniformity.

direct route, and just as it seems that they have developed the 'perfect' golf ball, they come up with another technical advance.

The modern two-piece ball is made of a solid rubber core, encased in a durable dimpled cover. The design and placement of the dimples is all important to the ball's trajectory and flight, therefore, the manufacturers are constantly experimenting with this area.

But how different it all was five hundred years ago when golf is believed to have started in earnest. Golf balls were originally made of wood, and inevitably without the machine tools of today they were not perfectly round. But at the turn of the seventeenth century the wooden ball gave way to the 'feathery', so-called because it was a cased leather ball stuffed with feathers.

A selection of gutta-percha and rubber-core balls. In the mid-nineteenth century the 'gutty' ball replaced the feathery. The 'gutty', made from a glue substance, could be moulded into a uniform round object.

Again, it was not fully rounded, and because it was hand-made, it lacked uniformity. Nevertheless, it provided extra length and as such was the first development in aiding the golfer with new equipment.

It was not until golf started becoming popular in the mid-nineteenth century that major strides forward were made, when the Reverend Robert Preston invented the 'gutty' ball. The 'gutty' was made of gutta-percha, a glue substance from Malaysia, which could be moulded into a uniform round object. It consequently became popular with the professionals of the day and for the first time they had the chance to demonstrate their skills by using a ball that rewarded accurate shots, rather than relying on the 'hit and miss' possibilities of the hand-made 'feathery'.

While the 'gutty' adopted a straight flight when hit correctly, it dropped out of the sky when it came to the end of its trajectory. However, it was soon realized that the 'gutty' travelled further towards the end of a round

of golf. This was the result of damage caused to the ball by contact with the clubhead. Manufacturers began experimenting by making 'damaged' balls. This led to the development of the dimpled ball, and later the 'Haskell' at the end of the nineteenth century, which went on to take golf ball design by storm.

The 'Haskell', so-called because it was invented by the American Coburn Haskell, was a three-piece, rubber-cored ball, wrapped around with elastic and coated in a dimpled plastic outer-casing. It took a while for his design to catch on with top professionals, but, after Sandy Herd outdrove his rivals to win the 1902 British Open, other professionals realized just how special the new ball was. The 'Haskell' with its dimples marked the first resemblance to the golf ball of today, although manufacturers have subsequently developed a two-piece ball, which has an acrylic cover over a single, central core.

The modern two-piece ball is made of a solid rubber core, encased in a durable dimpled cover.

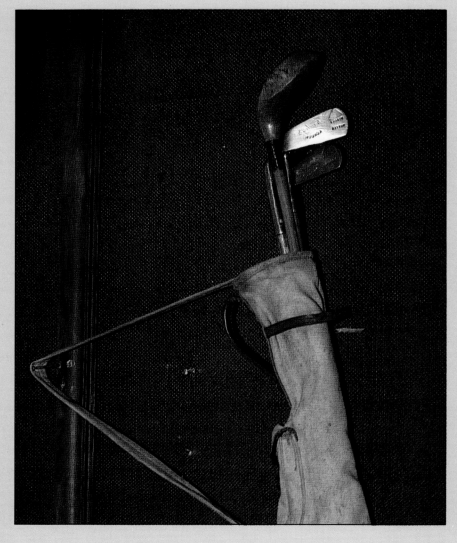

THE GOLF CLUB

Clubs have also come a long way from the earliest days when roughly hewn branches may have been used to knock around stones or wooden balls.

Early golf clubs were almost certainly made entirely of wood with the clubhead and shaft being made of different types, glued together and bound in twine. Hazel and ash were used for the shaft, while apple, beech, blackthorn and pear were popular for the head. The choice of wood also depended on the purpose of club, whether it was to be used for driving, fairway or approach play.

These clubs were satisfactory for use with the 'feathery' ball, but when the 'gutty' arrived in the mid-nineteenth century it put greater strain on them. Towards the end of the nineteenth century the golf club started to look very different, as an alternative wood, hickory, was used for the club shafts, and iron heads were developed to withstand the battering from the 'gutty', as well as to gain

A golf bag and clubs, from the beginning of the twentieth century.

A painting, c.1600, depicting the use of crude wooden clubs.

Old wooden clubs.

extra distance. It was also realized that clubs with different lofts could be used for different shots, and top players began carrying nine or ten clubs, as opposed to three or four.

While the wooden clubs could meet the demands of the 'gutty', they could not stand up to the 'Haskell' ball, and it was necessary to find a new material for clubheads. The North American wood, persimmon, was discovered to be ideal, but to prevent damage ivory or bone inserts were added to the clubface.

After World War I, hickory was in short supply, and it became necessary to seek an alternative material for the club shafts. Manufacturers turned to steel, and so the steel-shafted golf club was born. By the 1920s golf club manufacture had moved out of the hands of the individual craftsman and the mass-production of golf clubs was in full swing, so to speak!

Club sets now consisted of 14 clubs, and for the first time, players could buy a complete set of clubs that matched each other in style and design.

The steel-shafted clubs gave extra length and more control to the golf shot, yet manufacturers were still taking advantage of constantly improving technology to develop golf club design. Laminated plastic, and then light aluminium, replaced persimmon for use in clubheads, and graphite and titanium shafts were developed to enable more

movement of the clubhead through the ball. 'Cavity-back' clubs (irons with the cavity hollowed out of the back of the clubhead) have also been designed to give a more exact centre of gravity, to provide the golfer with a greater relationship with his club.

Computerized technology is now helping to advance the design of the golf club, giving golfers, both amateur and professional, equipment that will make their game that much easier, and even more enjoyable.

Modern cavity-back clubs showing the hollowed out clubhead. This gives a more exact centre of gravity.

THE GOLFING HALL OF FAME

For more than a century the game of golf has produced some of the best known personalities in the sporting world. Players such as Tiger Woods stand alongside other top-ranked world sportsmen for their earning capacity and endorsements. But Woods is just the latest in a long line of 'greats' that goes back to the days before championship golf when players like Allan Robertson were invincible.

Right, Tiger Woods

ALLAN ROBERTSON

Allan Robertson, whose death brought about the inaugural British Open Championship.

Mid-nineteenth century golfers; Allan Robertson is seventh from the left.

St Andrews-born Allan Robertson is widely regarded as the first true 'great' of the game of golf. He dominated the sport in the mid-nineteenth century and was almost invincible to such an extent that, following his death, a tournament was organized to find his successor as 'champion' golfer. And so was born the British Open Championship. It would have been interesting to see how he would have fared in championship conditions against the likes of Young and Old Tom Morris, Willie Park, Andrew Strath, and so on.

Robertson had golf in his veins from an early age and he helped run the family golf club and ball manufacturing business that overlooked St Andrews' 18th green. For a while Robertson's assistant was Old Tom Morris, and on the golf course the two men

were unbeatable; it is said that Robertson was never on the losing side in a four-man challenge match. He was one of the first players to realize the importance of playing accurate irons from fairway to green. Of the many matches Robertson and Morris played in together the most famous was against the Dunn brothers, Willie and Jamie. Played over 108 holes at three different links, the St Andrews pair trailed by four strokes with eight holes to play in the final match at North Berwick, but overcame the deficit to snatch a memorable and much-talked-about victory. Even after Morris and Robertson disagreed over business matters they still played together and remained unbeaten until Robertson's untimely death at the age of 44.

THE GREAT GOLFERS

Allan Robertson

Born St Andrews, Scotland, 1815. Dominated the sport in the mid-nineteenth century. The British Open was created the year after his death as a competition to find his successor as the greatest golfer. Died 1859.

Opposite: Nick Price.

TOM MORRIS SENIOR

Tom Morris Senior, or 'Old Tom' as he was affectionately known, was one of the first true greats of the game. He was runner-up to Willie Park in the very first British Open in 1860, but he then went on to capture four titles. Morris had already established himself as a golfing hero in the days before championship golf, as he and Allan Robertson were an almost invincible partnership.

It was only after Robertson's death that the Open was inaugurated to find his successor, and many felt the first 'champion' of golf would be Morris, but Park took that honour by two strokes. However, a year later Morris put the record straight by beating Park into second place by four strokes. Morris retained his title by 13 strokes, again with Park as runner-up, in 1862. Title number three came in 1864 and in 1867 he became the first man to win four titles. His

Old Tom Morris, one of the first greats of golf.

A painting of Old Tom Morris and Allan Robertson by Thomas Hodge.

son maintained the family tradition and became the next champion in 1868.

Old Tom Morris was the professional at Prestwick before returning to his native St Andrews to take his fourth title. He stayed there as head greenkeeper until 1904 when he was aged 83. Remarkably, he played in every British Open from 1860 until 1896 and when he captured the title in 1867 he became, and remains, the oldest winner of the championship. Old Tom Morris died in 1908 following a fall at the St Andrews clubhouse and the first great champion of golf was dead.

THE GREAT GOLFERS

Tom Morris, Snr.

Born St Andrews, Scotland, 1821. Runner-up in the first British Open and then went on to win the title four times – 1861, 1862, 1864 and 1867. He remains the oldest winner of this championship. Died 1908.

TOM MORRIS JUNIOR

Although it is not apparent from the record books, Young Tom Morris won four consecutive British Opens, a feat no man has managed to equal since. He won the title in the three years between 1868 and 1870, and again in 1872. There was no championship in 1871 because following his third win Morris was allowed to keep the trophy, the red Moroccan Belt, permanently. With no trophy to play for, the event was not held that year. The next year, when the British Open was revived with a new trophy, he became champion again.

Morris not only carried off four titles, but did so in record-breaking style and with scores that were unheard of in their day. He appeared in his first Open at the age of 14 in 1865 and when he captured his first title in 1868 he was only 17; to this day he remains the youngest champion. When he won his third title at 19 in 1870 he lowered the 36-hole championship record by five strokes, and his average of 74.5 strokes per round was not bettered until 1904. His opening round of 47 for Prestwick's 12 holes that year is regarded as one of the truly great rounds of championship golf.

Young Tom finished runner-up to Mungo Park at Musselburgh in 1874. Sadly it was to be the St Andrews man's last Open. Shortly before the 1875 championship, while playing a challenge match at North Berwick, he received a telegram saying his wife had been taken ill during childbirth. When he arrived at his St Andrews home both his wife and newborn baby had died. After a bout of heavy drinking and depression Young Tom died on Christmas Day. The golfing world mourned its finest player. He was only 24 years of age when he died but, in his all-too-brief career, he left a lasting mark on the game of golf.

THE GREAT GOLFERS

Tom Morris, Jnr.

Born St Andrews, Scotland, 1851. The greatest golfer of his generation. In a brief but brilliant career he won the British Open four times – 1868, 1869, 1870 and 1872. He is the youngest golfer ever to win the Championship. Died 1875.

Old and Young Tom Morris, c.1873.

Young Tom Morris sporting the red Moroccan Open Championship Belt which he won outright in 1870.

JOHN HENRY 'J.H.' TAYLOR

At the turn of the century British golf was dominated by three men, James Braid, Harry Vardon and the only English-born member of the 'Great Triumvirate', John Henry Taylor, known affectionately as 'J.H.'. The son of a Devon labourer, he left school at the age of 11 and after a succession of jobs joined the greenkeeping staff at Westward Ho! Golf Club, where his love affair with golf started.

Taylor turned professional at the age of 19 and became greenkeeper at nearby Burnham. Four years later, in 1894, he became the first non-Scottish-born winner of the British Open, when he won by five strokes at Sandwich. He was the first member of the 'Triumvirate' to win the title, and he retained it at St Andrews a year later with an equally convincing four-stroke margin. Vardon prevented a hat trick at Muirfield in 1896 however, when he won a play-off by four strokes. Title number three came Taylor's way at St Andrews in 1900 – it must have been sweet revenge because he won by a massive eight strokes from Vardon, thus preventing his rival from achieving a hat trick of wins. Taylor's fourth title was at Deal in 1909, he then equalled Braid and Vardon's five wins in 1913, achieving victory by eight strokes over Ted Ray.

Taylor played in the British Open for far longer than his two rivals, and was still competing 30 years after his first triumph. Most of Taylor's professional career was spent at the Royal Mid-Surrey Club, and off the golf course he played a large part in the formation of the Professional Golfers' Association (PGA).

A painting of the 'Triumvirate'.

J.H. Taylor after capturing the 1894 British Open.

HARRY VARDON

Harry Vardon was the most successful of the 'Great Triumvirate' with six British Open titles and one US Open title to his credit. But his win in the USA in 1900 did more than add a piece of silverware to the Vardon mantelpiece; it helped arouse great interest in the game on the American side of the Atlantic where golf was still, to a certain extent, in its infancy. By then, the former caddy had started establishing himself as one of the next golfing greats.

Vardon came to England from Jersey in 1890 and appeared in the British Open three years later. However, he did not capture the first of his

Right: Vardon, the most prolific champion in British Open history. Seen here in action in 1900, by which time he had already won the title three times.

Far right: A cigarette card depicting Vardon, c. 1912.

record-breaking six titles until 1896 when he beat J.H. Taylor, one of his fellow members of the 'Triumvirate' by four strokes in a play-off. Back-to-back wins came in 1898 and 1899, but Taylor thwarted a hat trick at St Andrews in 1900. Vardon made amends by beating Taylor into second place in the US Open at Chicago.

Vardon won his third British Open in 1903 (when he beat his brother Tom into second place), but he had an eight-year wait before equalling James Braid's record of five titles, when he beat the Frenchman Arnaud Massy in a play-off at Sandwich. Vardon came close to a second US Open title in 1913 but was beaten in a play-off by the unknown US amateur Francis Ouimet. This was a win that changed the face of golf in America because Ouimet inspired many new golfers.

A year later Vardon recaptured the British Open at Prestwick. It was the 16th and last title for the 'Triumvirate', and Vardon's sixth. No other player has won so many Open titles.

THE GREAT GOLFERS

Harry Vardon

Born Jersey, Channel Islands, 1870. The most successful of the Triumvirate, he won the British Open a record six times between 1896 and 1914 and the US Open in 1900. Vardon did much to increase the popularity of golf, particularly in America. Died 1937.

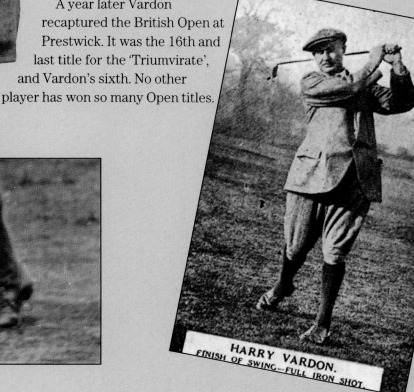

HARRY VARDON.
FINISH OF SWING—FULL IRON SHOT.

JAMES BRAID

James Braid was one of the three members of the 'Great Triumvirate' which dominated British golf at the turn of the century, winning 16 British Open titles between them; the other members were Harry Vardon and J.H. Taylor. Braid captured five titles, the first at Muirfield in 1901 when he beat Vardon by three shots. A professional for eight years at the time, he had been threatening to capture the title since finishing second to Harold Hilton at Hoylake in 1897. When Braid won his second title, at St Andrews in 1905, it was Taylor, and Rolland Jones who trailed by five strokes. A four-stroke victory over Taylor ensured Braid retained the title at Muirfield in 1906 and two years later at Prestwick he won his fourth title. His score of 291 for the 72 holes was to remain an Open record until surpassed by the great Bobby Jones in 1927. When Braid won the Open at St Andrews in

James Braid on his way to winning his first British Open at Muirfield, in 1901.

A commemorative postcard to celebrate the fiftieth British Open at St Andrews.

1910 by beating Sandy Herd by four shots, he became the first man to win the title five times. Only Harry Vardon has won more British Opens.

After his retirement James Braid was involved in golf course design and applied his skills to such courses as Carnoustie, Royal Blackheath and Gleneagles. The golfing world lost one of its true greats when James Braid died in 1950 at the age of 80.

THE GREAT GOLFERS

James Braid

Born Earlsferry, Scotland, 1870. The third member of the Triumvirate, Braid won the British Open in 1901 and went on to claim four more titles in 1905, 1906, 1908 and 1910. He was one of the founders of the PGA and designed the Kings Course at Gleneagles. Died 1950.

TED RAY

Ted Ray had the misfortune of being around at the same time as golf's 'Great Triumvirate'. Nevertheless, he managed to break through the stranglehold they had on the game and when he won the British Open in 1912 his victory was warmly greeted by fans and fellow professionals alike, including the 'Triumvirate' themselves.

Like Harry Vardon, Ray was born in Jersey, and also like Vardon, he was the professional at Ganton in Yorkshire, England, for a while. He first made an impression when he finished runner-up to James Braid in the 1901 *News of the World* tournament. In 1912, Ray — instantly recognizable by his battered homburg, and pipe constantly in his mouth — won the British Open when he beat Vardon by four strokes at Muirfield. The following year he was beaten into second place by J.H. Taylor and that same year Ray finished third in the US Open at Brookline, after a play-off involving Vardon and the unknown American amateur, Francis Ouimet. But in 1920 Ray became the first British winner of the US title since Harry Vardon in 1900, and the oldest winner at 43, when he beat Vardon and three Americans into second place by one stroke at the Inverness Club, Ohio.

Ray last came close to winning the British Open in 1925, when he was runner-up with Archie Compston, behind Jim Barnes. Two years later he was honoured with the Ryder Cup captaincy. He died in 1943.

Ted Ray, winner of the US Open in 1920. This was the last British win until Jacklin's victory 50 years later.

THE GREAT GOLFERS

Ted Ray

Born Jersey, Channel Islands, 1877. Ted Ray won the British Open in 1912 and US Open in 1920. Ray was a great golfer, who had a fine swing, but his career was overshadowed by the 'Triumvirate'. Died 1943.

The moment that changed the course of golfing history. Ouimet on the 18th green with Vardon and Ray in the US Open at Brookline, 1913. Ouimet's victory ushered in a period of American success in championship golf.

WALTER HAGEN

The flamboyant Hagen always attracted a large gallery.

THE GREAT GOLFERS

Walter Hagen

Born Rochester, New York, 1892. Hagen's 11 Major victories marked the beginning of a period in which the Americans dominated championship golf for 20 years. In 1922 he became the first American-born winner of the British Open. Died 1969.

Walter Hagen after winning his third British Open title.

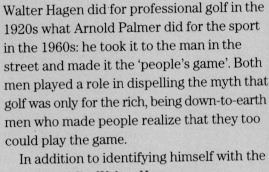

Walter Hagen did for professional golf in the 1920s what Arnold Palmer did for the sport in the 1960s: he took it to the man in the street and made it the 'people's game'. Both men played a role in dispelling the myth that golf was only for the rich, being down-to-earth men who made people realize that they too could play the game.

In addition to identifying himself with the general public, Walter Hagen was a flamboyant character and one who brought a great deal of flair and colour into the game.

A former caddie, Hagen attracted attention soon after turning professional and his skilful putting, together with his carefree approach, started winning him tournaments as well as admirers. He became the first great American golfer of the 1920s.

Having won the US Open in 1914 and 1919, and the US PGA title in 1921, Hagen captured the British Open at Sandwich in 1922 and became the first American-born winner of the title. After finishing second to Arthur Havers at Troon in 1923 he regained the title in 1924. He followed this Open success by winning the first of four consecutive US PGA titles, in the days when it was played under match-play rules, and he certainly earned a reputation as one of the greatest match-play golfers ever. Back-to-back British Opens followed in 1928 and 1929 as he took his tally of professional Majors to 11, a figure bettered only by Jack Nicklaus.

Hagen died at Traverse City, Michigan in 1969 at the age of 76.

Portrait of Hagen by Frank Bensinge, 1957.

GENE SARAZEN

Gene Sarazen was involved in two of golf's most talked about incidents, and they came 38 years apart. The first was at Augusta during the final round of the 1935 Masters which he won after a play-off against Craig Wood. To get into the play-off, Sarazen holed out a 2-wood from the fairway at the par 5 15th for an albatross (double eagle). It remains one of the most talked-about golf shots in Augusta, Georgia.

The second of Sarazen's memorable shots was at Troon in 1973 when he holed in one at the short 8th Postage Stamp hole in front of millions of television viewers. Sarazen was 71 at the time. Ironically, his first trip to Britain for the British Open 50 years earlier, was also at Troon, but he failed to qualify.

However, in between the two appearances the little man made a great impact on the game and carried off all of its major honours and titles. He won both the US Open and US PGA titles in 1922, retained the PGA a year later, and in 1932 he carried off another double when he won the US and British Open titles to become the first professional to win both titles in the same year. He won his third PGA in 1933 and two years later he became the first man to win all four Majors when he won the second Masters title, thanks to that double eagle! Sarazen won no more Majors after that but continued playing successfully on the US Tour, winning a total of 38 events.

Gene Sarazen

Born Harrison, New York, 1902. Sarazen won his first Major, the US Open in 1922. In 1935, when he won the Masters, he became the first player to win all four Majors.

Sarazen at the Masters. He was the first man to win all four Majors.

At the 1973 British Open. The day before he had scored an ace.

183

BOBBY JONES

Robert 'Bobby' Tyre Jones never turned professional during his all-too-brief career, but that did not prevent him from taking on and beating all the top professionals of the 1920s. He rightly earned himself the title of 'greatest amateur golfer of all time'. One could probably delete the word 'amateur' from that title and there would be very few who would argue.

Jones graduated from college with degrees in law, literature and engineering. He was already a very talented golfer, and the world was his oyster. He chose law as his profession with golf as his great hobby. He developed one of the finest swings ever seen, and it was that swing which helped take him to the top.

Jones won his first Major in 1923 when he won the US Open after a play-off. The following year he won the first of two successive US Amateur titles. He won both the US and British Open in 1926 and in 1927 he retained his British Open title at St Andrews and made it another double by

Bobby Jones taking his final drive to win another US Open at Winged Foot, 1929.

Portrait of Bobby Jones by J.A.A. Berrie.

taking the US Amateur title for the third time. He made it four the following year and in 1929 he maintained his winning streak by capturing the US Open after a 36-hole play-off with Al Espinosa at Winged Foot. That took Jones' record to nine amateur and professional Majors in seven years, playing against top professionals like Walter Hagen and Gene Sarazen.

However, the best was still to come because in 1930 Jones first won the British Amateur title at St Andrews, then took the British Open at Hoylake, returned to America to take his fourth US Open and then, on 27 September 1930, completed the game's most remarkable Grand Slam when he added the US Amateur title by beating Eugene Homans 8 & 7 in the final at Merion. On this triumphant note Bobby Jones decided to retire from competitive golf at the age of 28. His career might have lasted only eight years but he certainly left his mark on the game.

And after he finished playing Jones further ensured his place in the game's hall of fame by giving golf one of its finest courses, the Augusta National, and also the Masters, the great championship which is played there every April. Jones died in his native Georgia on 18 December 1971.

Bobby Jones

Born Atlanta, Georgia, 1902. Jones, the greatest amateur, was the idol of the ordinary golfer. In a short, brilliant career he won the US Open four times and the British Open three times. He retired aged 28 but went on to build Augusta National. Died 1971.

HENRY COTTON

Henry Cotton's contribution to the game of golf is a huge one. Not only was he an outstanding golfer both before and after World War II, but he was the inspiration for many up-and-coming young British golfers in the 1950s; in the 30 years following his retirement from competitive golf he spent much of his time encouraging and developing the skills of young golfers.

Cotton turned professional at the age of 17 and at 19 was appointed professional at Langley Park. He was a member of the successful British Ryder Cup team of 1929, and in 1947 and 1953 he was honoured with the team's captaincy.

Cotton's domination of European golf started when he captured the Belgian Open in 1930 and it was while he was the professional at Belgium's Waterloo Club that

Cotton captured his first British Open at Sandwich in 1934; his second-round 65 remained an Open record until bettered by Mark Hayes at Turnberry 43 years later. Back in England, Cotton captured his second Open title at Carnoustie in 1937 and he became the only man to win the title both before and after World War II when he beat defending champion Fred Daly by five strokes at Muirfield in 1948.

During the war Cotton served with the RAF, but was invalided out because of ulcers and a burst appendix. He put his skills to good use by raising money for the Red Cross and was later rewarded with the MBE. Cotton spent much of his retirement in his beloved Portugal before his death in 1987.

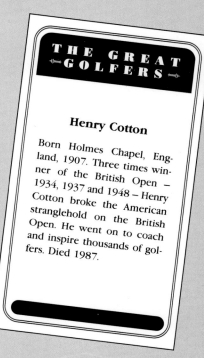

THE GREAT GOLFERS

Henry Cotton

Born Holmes Chapel, England, 1907. Three times winner of the British Open – 1934, 1937 and 1948 – Henry Cotton broke the American stranglehold on the British Open. He went on to coach and inspire thousands of golfers. Died 1987.

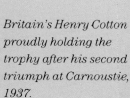

Henry Cotton was an inspiration to many young golfers in the 1950s.

Britain's Henry Cotton proudly holding the trophy after his second triumph at Carnoustie, 1937.

SAM SNEAD

No man has won more events on the US Tour than 'Slammin' Sam Snead. His total of 81 wins between 1936 and 1965 is 11 more than second-placed Jack Nicklaus. But remarkably, the man who won around 135 tournaments world-wide, including seven Majors, never won the US Open, the one title he so desperately wanted. He was runner-up on four occasions, including his début in 1937, three years after he turned professional.

Snead's first Tour win was in the 1936 Virginia Closed Championship and his 81st, and last, was in the Greensboro Open – at the age of 52 years and 10 months he became the oldest-ever Tour winner. In the early

SAM SNEAD
PROFESSIONAL GOLF STAR

Sam Snead receiving the silver claret jug after winning his first and only British Open.

The most successful professional golfer, Snead won 81 US Tour events.

post-war years, Snead, Ben Hogan and Byron Nelson dominated golf in the United States.

Sam won seven Majors. His first was in 1942 when he beat Jim Turnesa 2 & 1 to win the US PGA title. Four years later he won the first post-war British Open at St Andrews but his glory years were between 1949 and 1954 when he won the Masters three times and US PGA title twice. When he won his last Major, the 1954 Masters, he did so at the age of 41 years 11 months – the oldest winner of the title at that time. Sam was still winning money on the Regular Tour up to 1979.

BEN HOGAN

Ben Hogan rightly takes his place as one of the true greats of the game of golf. Born in Texas in 1912, he turned professional in 1931 but had to wait seven years for his first tournament success. But once it came, in the 1938 Hershey Fourball, it was the springboard for greater things as he became one of the outstanding golfers in the immediate post-war years.

It was in the 1946 US PGA Championship that Hogan captured his first Major and over the next three seasons he won no fewer than 31 tournaments. He regained the US PGA title in 1948 and won the first of four US Open titles that same year. But 1949 nearly proved to be a disastrous year following a bad

car accident. Hogan was at first presumed dead but he survived only to be told that he would never play golf again and would probably not even walk again. Eleven months later he took part in the Los Angeles Open and 16 months after his horrific accident he won the fiftieth US Open at Merion after a play-off. It was a remarkable achievement.

Hogan went on to win the US Open again, and the Masters, in 1951 and then came a truly memorable season in 1953 when he won three of the four Majors. Had the British Open and US PGA Championship not clashed he may well have won all four. To this day no other man has won three Majors in one season.

Hogan kept on playing and in the 1967 Masters he shot a third-round 66 at the age of 54, reminding people of his great talent.

THE GREAT GOLFERS

Ben Hogan

Born Fort Worth, Texas, 1912. Considered by many to be the greatest golfer of the modern era, Hogan dominated the American game after World War II, winning the US Open four times, the Masters and the US PGA twice, and the British Open once.

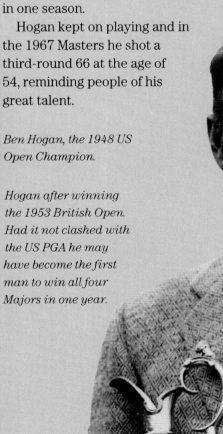

Ben Hogan, the 1948 US Open Champion.

Hogan after winning the 1953 British Open. Had it not clashed with the US PGA he may have become the first man to win all four Majors in one year.

BOBBY LOCKE

A former bomber pilot from South Africa, Bobby Locke, dominated the British Open Championship in the late 1940s and 1950s, along with Australia's Peter Thomson. They won the title nine times between them. Locke was readily identifiable on the golf course with his famous plus-fours and white cap.

A professional since 1938, he travelled to Britain after the war to develop his skills alongside the best of the British professionals, and in the first post-war Open, at St Andrews in 1946, he finished runner-up to Sam Snead. He then tried his hand across the Atlantic and in 1947 won seven tournaments. The following year he won the Chicago Victory National by a record 16 strokes. His first British Open title

came when he beat Harry Bradshaw in a play-off at Sandwich in 1949, and the following year he beat Argentina's Roberto de Vicenzo by two strokes at Troon. Locke beat his great rival Thomson to win his third title at Lytham in 1952 and it was Thomson again who came home second to the South African when Locke won his fourth Open at St Andrews in 1957.

Locke won more than 80 tournaments world-wide, the last being on home soil in the 1958 Transvaal Open. A car accident damaged his eyesight in 1960 and he played little competitive golf thereafter.

Locke, the first great South African golfer and inspiration to the likes of Gary Player.

Locke, distinguishable in his plus-fours and white cap.

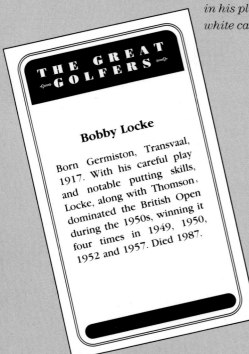

THE GREAT GOLFERS

Bobby Locke

Born Germiston, Transvaal, 1917. With his careful play and notable putting skills, Locke, along with Thomson, dominated the British Open during the 1950s, winning it four times in 1949, 1950, 1952 and 1957. Died 1987.

PETER THOMSON

The 1980s saw an abundance of talented golfers emerge from Australia but none could achieve what their fellow countryman Peter Thomson did in the 1950s when he attained a twentieth-century record of five British Open titles. He would be the first to admit that he never had the competition that his fellow countrymen face these days, but that should not detract from the fact that he achieved a record unparalleled since the days of the 'Great Triumvirate'. Thomson's three successive wins between 1954 and 1956 had not been achieved since Young Tom Morris 80 years earlier.

Thomson turned professional in 1950 and immediately went on to win his first professional tournament, the New Zealand Open – an impressive start to a career! He won that title nine times and the Australian Open three times; the last being in 1972 at the age of 43.

But it was after making the journey to Europe that Thomson really made his mark. He first competed in the Open in 1951 and finished sixth. But over the next eight years he had a remarkable record. He lost by one stroke to South Africa's Bobby Locke in 1952, was fourth in 1953, but then won Birkdale's first Open in 1954. He retained his title at St Andrews a year later and completed the hat trick at Hoylake in 1956. He was runner-up to Locke again in 1957, but it was back to winning ways for the Australian in 1958 when he beat Britain's Dave Thomas in a play-off at Lytham. Just when it looked as though the winning had stopped, Thomson beat the UK pair of Christy O'Connor and Brian Huggett to win at Birkdale for a second time in 1965. Remarkably, four of Thomson's British Open wins were on English soil.

Thomson tried his hand on the US Tour in the 1950s but his long-iron play was not suited to the American courses. However, when he joined the Seniors' Tour in 1979 his fortunes were reversed and he started winning money on a scale undreamt of in his youth. He was made an honorary member of the Royal and Ancient Golf Club in 1982.

Two of the top golfers of the 1950s, Locke (left) and Thomson (right).

THE GREAT GOLFERS

Peter Thomson

Born Melbourne, Australia, 1929. The most successful Australian golfer in Major championship history, Thomson won the British Open five times – 1954, 1955, 1956, 1958 and 1965 – and he is the only player to have won a hat trick this century.

Peter Thomson during the 1956 British Open. He went on to win his third title; the first and only hat trick this century.

THE GOLFING HALL OF FAME

ARNOLD PALMER

Arnold Palmer

Born Latrobe, Pennsylvania, 1929. Palmer won seven Majors between 1958 and 1964, but he is also renowned as the first great media star of golf. With his exciting, big-hitting style he won the hearts of millions.

Arnold Palmer on his way to victory at the British Open, in 1961.

Soon after his arrival on the golfing scene in the mid-1950s Arnold Palmer became one of the most popular golfers world-wide. He did what few had done before, and took the game to ordinary people. His enthusiasm for the sport was infectious and he was largely responsible for television and sponsors turning their attention to golf. His success made more people aware of the game all over the world, and, thanks partly to the Arnold Palmer driving ranges, people took up this great game by the millions.

Palmer won the US Amateur title in 1954 and turned professional a year later. Before the year was out he had captured the first of his 61 US Tour titles – the Canadian Open, regarded by many as the 'Fifth Major'. The first of his Majors came in 1958 when he won the Masters. Two years later he won both the Masters and US Open, though only after the amateur Jack Nicklaus had given him a scare.

Arnie won the first of two back-to-back British Open titles in 1961, and played a large part in encouraging his fellow American professionals to make the trip across the Atlantic to the world's greatest golf tournament. American interest in the British Open had been on the decline in the 1950s but Palmer's support for and participation in that great tournament ensured its pre-eminence in the golfing world.

Arnold Palmer never won the US PGA title but added two more Masters titles to his honours when he won in 1962 and 1964. His last victory on the regular US Tour was in 1973 when he won the Bob Hope Desert Classic, but he continues to thrill his army of fans wherever he plays.

The winning ways returned in 1979 after Arnold Palmer joined the Seniors Tour and it is now like 'old times' with Nicklaus, Player and Trevino all joining Arnie in renewal of their rivalry of a quarter of a century ago.

Above: Arnold Palmer playing from the rough, 1991.

Below: Arnold Palmer and Casper at the 1966 US Open.

GARY PLAYER

South Africa's Gary Player epitomizes all that is good about sport. His manners are exemplary and his sportsmanship second-to-none and he has won trophies in all parts of the world.

Gary turned professional at the age of 17 in 1953 and two years later won his first professional title, in Egypt. He made his British début in 1956 and won the Dunlop Tournament at Sunningdale. A year later he made his way to America and became just as successful and popular there. The first of 21 US Tour event wins, the most by a non-American, came in the 1958 Kentucky Derby Open, and a year later he won his first Major when he took the British Open at Muirfield.

Gary Player became the first non-American winner of the Masters in 1961 and a little over 12 months later he also became the first overseas winner of the US PGA title. He completed the 'Grand Slam' of all four Majors in 1965 when

The 1974 British Open was the first time the larger American ball was compulsory.

he won the US Open after a play-off with Australia's Kel Nagle. He also won the first of his record five world match-play titles at Wentworth that year. He beat Bob Charles and Jack Nicklaus to win the British Open at Carnoustie in 1968 and in 1972 he won a second US PGA title. But he saved his best for 1974 when he won his second Masters and then beat Britain's Peter Oosterhuis to win the British Open at Lytham. Even that great year was later overshadowed by his third Masters success in 1978 when he came from nowhere to win the title at the age of 42. At the start of the final round he wasn't even a contender but seven birdies in the last ten holes soon improved his chances.

Gary Player continues to enjoy himself on the Seniors Tour with his old buddies, like Jack Nicklaus.

THE GREAT GOLFERS

Gary Player

Born Johannesburg, South Africa, 1935. Gary Player, a golfer dedicated to fitness and training, won the British Open and the Masters three times between 1959 and 1978, the US PGA in 1962 and 1972, and the US Open in 1965.

Gary Player giving it his all, c. 1964.

JACK NICKLAUS

The amateur Jack Nicklaus in 1960.

All the superlatives have been used to describe Jack Nicklaus. He is, quite simply, one of the all-time greats of the game of golf. His potential was revealed to the American public when he won the 1959 US Amateur title at 19 and then finished second to the great Arnold Palmer in the 1960 US Open. It took a brilliant 65 from Palmer in the last round to thwart the challenge of the amateur Nicklaus. Jack went on to capture his second amateur title in 1961. Further honours soon followed after he turned professional in 1962 and his first win as a paid member of the US Tour was in that year's Open at Oakmont, when he beat Palmer in a play-off. That was to be the first of a record-breaking 18 professional Majors for 'The Golden Bear', as he went on to become the greatest modern-day golfer. He went on to win the US Open on three more occasions, in 1967, 1972 and 1980. He won the US PGA title in 1963, 1971, 1973, 1975 and 1980. And he gained many friends on the British side of the Atlantic by winning the British Open on three occasions, the first at his beloved Muirfield in 1966. Other triumphs followed in 1970 and 1978.

It was in the Masters at Augusta that Jack enjoyed some of his greatest moments. Having won his first Masters in 1963 he became the first man to win back-to-back titles in 1965 and 1966. There were three more titles still to come, but after winning in 1972 and 1975 it seemed that was the end of his Augusta glory days. But no; he became the oldest-ever Masters champion at the age of 46 when he recaptured the cherished title in 1986, confirming that he was still a great player and should never be written off.

But it is not only in Majors that Nicklaus has enjoyed enormous success. His total of 70 regular Tour wins is second only to Sam Snead's all-time record. Furthermore, Jack has been runner-up on the US Tour an amazing 58 times. In addition, he was top money winner eight times, US PGA Player of the Year five times, a member of five Ryder Cup teams, and non-playing captain twice, appeared on six winning US World Cup teams and much more.

Upon reaching the age of 50, Jack joined the US Seniors Tour, renewing his rivalry with some of the great names of the 1960s, notably Arnold Palmer and Gary Player.

Jack Nicklaus during the 1977 British Open at Turnberry.

LEE TREVINO

Lee Trevino was born in the Texan city of Dallas to Mexican parents in 1939. From a poor and humble background he went on to be one of the best-loved golfers in the world. One of the great characters of the game and a journalists' dream, Trevino's wit and humour always provided them with a laugh and good quote.

He started caddying at a local course at the age of eight and although he did not start playing straight away, he studied the scientific principles of the game by observing the players. By the time he was 14 he wanted nothing other than to play golf.

Completely self-taught, Trevino turned professional in 1960, yet it took eight years before his first Tour win. But only 'Super Mex' could have had his first Tour win in the US Open at Oak Hill. He went on to win 27

Trevino and Mr Lu of Taiwan after they had engaged in a memorable final round in the British Open.

Lee Trevino has always been one of golf's great characters.

Tour events and represent his country in six Ryder Cup matches. Sadly he was the non-playing captain in 1985 when the United States lost for the first time in 28 years.

Lee Trevino has delighted the British fans for many years, not least at Birkdale when winning the 1971 British Open after a great contest with Mr Lu and Britain's Tony Jacklin. He retained his title at Muirfield a year later, when he destroyed Jacklin's chances again by holing two chip shots and one shot from a bunker, ensuring his victory. His 1971 British Open success was part of a remarkable triple which saw him capture the US, British and Canadian Opens all within 21 days.

In addition to winning the Open titles of Britain and America he also won the US PGA title twice, in 1974 and 1984. However, he has never won the Masters.

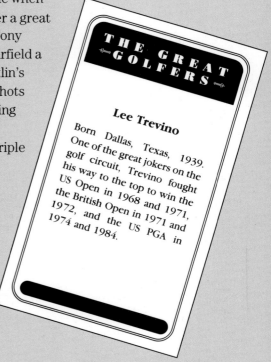

THE GREAT GOLFERS

Lee Trevino

Born Dallas, Texas, 1939. One of the great jokers on the golf circuit, Trevino fought his way to the top to win the US Open in 1968 and 1971, the British Open in 1971 and 1972, and the US PGA in 1974 and 1984.

TOM WATSON

THE GREAT GOLFERS

Tom Watson

Born Kansas City, Texas, 1949. With five British Open victories, Watson only needs one more to equal Vardon's record. Also having won the Masters twice and the US Open once, he has been one of the most feared golfers of the 70s and 80s.

In the decade between the mid-1970s and mid-1980s, Tom Watson was one of the most feared golfers both sides of the Atlantic. On British soil he emulated Peter Thomson's post-war record of five British Open titles. And with the way he has performed in this Championship in recent years he may still win an all-time record-equalling sixth title.

Since winning the first of more than 30 US Tour events, the 1974 Western Open, Watson was tipped as the successor to Jack Nicklaus. And while he never quite toppled the great man or came near to his records, there were times when Watson certainly had the upper hand. Their great duel at Turnberry's first British Open in 1977, when they shattered all previous British Open records, was one of the truly memorable clashes in world golf.

The first of Watson's eight Majors was in 1975 when he beat the unfortunate Australian Jack Newton in a play-off over Carnoustie's monster course. He completed the Masters/British Open double in 1977 and on both occasions he had the satisfaction of seeing Nicklaus take second place. He won his third British Open at Muirfield in 1980 and when he took his second Masters title in 1981 Nicklaus was the runner-up. Nicklaus had to be content with second place to Watson again in the 1982 US Open at Pebble Beach which Watson won by chipping in from rough just off the green at the 17th on the final day. Watson won his fourth British Open, at Troon, that year to become only the fifth man to win both titles in the same year. He equalled Peter Thomson's post-war record a year later when he won the British Open on English soil for the first time, beating Hale Irwin and Andy Bean by one stroke at Birkdale.

In 1989 Watson was one stroke off the lead going into the final round at Troon, but a closing 72 meant he just missed the three-way play-off. But such is his love of the British Open that he will keep trying to achieve that magical sixth win.

Tom Watson savours the moment of success after taking his fifth British Open title at Birkdale, 1983.

Records galore were broken at the British Open, 1977.

SEVERIANO BALLESTEROS

Unquestionably the finest golfer produced by Spain, Seve shot to the forefront of world golf in 1976 when he emerged as a challenger for the British Open title as a 19-year-old, only to share second place with Jack Nicklaus behind Johnny Miller at Birkdale. But the name of Severiano Ballesteros was firmly implanted on the minds of the fans. From there he went on to top the European money list. His first Major was in 1979 when he won the British Open at Lytham with Ben Crenshaw and Jack Nicklaus sharing second place. He became the youngest winner of the Masters the following year and he regained this title in 1983 with a four-shot victory. He beat Tom Watson and Bernhard Langer to capture his second British Open title at St Andrews in 1984 and his third Open victory

Seve Ballesteros putting during the 1989 Ryder Cup, at the Belfry.

Seve Ballesteros is the youngest of four brothers who are all top-quality golfers.

was again at Lytham, in 1988.

A stalwart of the successful European Ryder Cup team in the 1980s, Seve has also won a record-equalling five World match-play titles, has won more than 50 titles world-wide, and has collected more than £3 million in prize-money during his career.

Seve comes from a family with a fine golfing tradition: his uncle Ramon Sota finished sixth in the 1965 Masters behind Jack Nicklaus, and Seve's brothers, Manuel, Baldomero and Vicente, are all top-quality golfers. The family has a long history of sporting successes as his father, another Baldomero, was a long-distance runner and top-class rower who won several national titles.

THE GREAT GOLFERS

Severiano Ballesteros

Born Pedrena, Spain, 1957. With his swash-buckling style, Seve Ballesteros is undoubtedly the best golfer to have come from Spain. He won the British Open in 1979, 1984 and 1988 and the Masters in 1980 and 1983.

TOM KITE

One of the biggest money winners on the US Tour, Tom Kite became the first man to amass $6 million in prize-money in August 1990 when he won the Federal Express St Jude Classic at Memphis. He went on to win over $7 million and in 1992 he eventually threw away the tag of 'being the best golfer never to win a Major' when he captured the US Open at Pebble Beach. Having been runner-up in the Masters in 1983 and 1986, when Jack Nicklaus captured the title with a brilliant final-round 66, and again in the

THE GREAT GOLFERS

Tom Kite

Born Austin, Texas, 1949. The top money winner in American golfing history, Kite looked like going through his career without a Major until he won the US Open in 1992. Putting is one of the strongest elements of his game.

Tom Kite in action during the 1989 Dunhill Cup.

Tom Kite won the US Open in 1992, ending his jinx in Majors.

British Open in 1978, when it was Nicklaus again who beat him to the title, it finally all came right for the likeable Texan at Pebble Beach in 1992.

A former US Amateur Championship runner-up (he was second to Lanny Wadkins in 1970), Kite represented his country in the Walker Cup before turning professional. He was the PGA's Rookie of the Year in 1973. His subsequent high earnings have come about due to very consistent golf which has seen him win more than 15 US titles. He has also been honoured with the coveted Bob Jones Award, the PGA Player of the Year title, and the Ryder Cup.

NICK FALDO

Nick Faldo was unquestionably the world's greatest golfer in the second half of the 1980s and he carried that tag into the 1990s. He emerged as a potential champion in 1975 when he captured the English Amateur title at the age of 18 and two years later he was the youngest member of the British Ryder Cup team. Rookie of the Year in 1977, he went on to win the PGA title three times between 1978 and 1981.

However, despite being consistently amongst the top money winners, Faldo was keen to better himself and at the end of the 1983 season went to coach David Leadbetter for assistance in re-building his swing. People told Nick he was mad. But one only has to look at his record since then to know the decision was fully justified. He won on American soil for the first time in 1984 when he took the Sea Pines Heritage Classic, and in 1987 he captured the British Open at Muirfield when America's Paul Azinger handed the title to him on a plate. But three years later he needed no such generosity when he won at St Andrews by five shots. In between his two British Open wins, Faldo became the first man since Jack Nicklaus to win back-to-back Masters titles, with victory coming at the second extra play-off hole in each case.

Since 1990, Faldo has gone on to win a third British Open title, the first Briton to do so in the post-war years.

It may have been Nick Faldo's third British Open, but it was equally as enjoyable as the other two, 1992.

THE GREAT GOLFERS

Nick Faldo

Born Welwyn Garden City, England, 1957. Nick Faldo became the world's number one golfer in the latter half of the 80s and 90s. His three British Opens and two Masters make him the most successful British golfer of the twentieth century.

BERNHARD LANGER

A professional since 1972, Bernhard Langer has been the most successful German golfer ever and has won well over 30 tournaments in more than a dozen countries, including the United States, where he was the Masters champion in 1985.

In the 1980s, Langer vied with Severiano Ballesteros as the leading European golfer and in 1981 and 1984 he toppled the Spaniard from the top of the European money-list. Since winning his first major title, the Cacharel Under-25s Championship by 17 strokes in 1979, he has been one of the top money winners in Europe and his career earnings have topped the £2 million mark.

Bernhard enjoyed one of his proudest moments in golf in 1981 when he became the first German to win the German Open, and that same year he finished second to Bill Rogers in the British Open. He was runner-up, to Ballesteros, in 1984, but has not come so close to winning the title since.

Langer's solitary Major came in 1985 when he came from six behind at the half-way stage to take the Masters from Ballesteros, Curtis Strange and Raymond Floyd after two brilliant rounds of 68. A week later he enjoyed back-to-back US wins when he took the Sea Pines Heritage Classic at Hilton Head after beating Bobby Wadkins in a play-off. Sadly for

Bernhard he was struck down with the dreaded putting ailment, 'the yips', in the late 1980s and it took a couple of years for him to get the problem sorted out. But he has now returned to his winning ways and is again one of the top golfers in Europe.

Bernhard Langer during the Ryder Cup, 1989.

THE GREAT GOLFERS

Bernhard Langer

Born Anhausen, Germany, 1957. The best golfer ever produced by Germany, Langer has enjoyed enormous success on both sides of the Atlantic and is popular with the American fans. He won the Masters in 1985.

At one time Europe's number one, Langer has recently shown that he is making progress towards regaining the top slot.

Tiger Woods

Tiger Woods is the world's number 1 golfer. After dominating the amateur game and turning professional Woods has won 10 major championships including The Masters (1997, 2001, 2002, 2005), The US Open (2000, 2002), The USPGA (1999, 2000) and The British Open (2000, 2005).

Tiger has thrilled audiences worldwide with his skills by winning three consecutive major championships and career grand slam, nine PGA Tour victories and single-season earnings record of US$ 8,286,821. Tiger also has the longest record streak of 142-consecutive cuts on the PGA Tour.

In 2004 he set the record for most weeks as No.1 in the World Ranking with 32 weeks at the top. His first Masters win in 1997 rewrote the record books when he became the youngest champion and also recorded the lowest total of 270.

He is a renowned long driver but also has an amazing short game and delicate touch around the greens which helped him win his second British Open Championship by four shots at St Andrews in July 2005.

Above, Tiger wins for the second time at the 2005 British Open at St Andrews.

Below, Tiger during his first British Open at St Andrews in 2000.

THE GREAT GOLFERS

Tiger Woods

Born 1975 - Eldrick 'Tiger' Woods in Cypress, California.

Tiger Woods is one of the greatest golfers the world has ever seen. At the age of thirty he has achieved what many golfers have only ever dreamed about. He is renowned for the power and length of his hitting, the imagination of his recovery strokes and the accuracy of his putting.

THE GREAT WOMEN GOLFERS

While it is only in more modern times that the ladies' professional game has flourished, women have been playing competitive golf as long as their male counterparts. In Babe Zaharias, the world of sport not only saw one of the finest lady golfers of all-time, but one of the world's great all-round athletes. But she is just one of the many women who can rightly stake a claim as one of golf's greats.

MILDRED ZAHARIAS

Born Mildred Didrikson, she was known affectionately as 'Babe' because of her adoration for baseball legend Babe Ruth. After graduating from high school, Mildred won national honours as a basketball player but before the 1932 Olympics she competed in the National Track and Field Championships. She won six of the eight events she entered and set three world records.

Mildred was, understandably, selected for the Olympics, but each competitor was only allowed to enter three events. She won two of her three, and with record-breaking performances. Her golds came in the hurdles and javelin but she was disqualified from first place in the high jump because of her then illegal 'Western Roll'. However, she was allowed to keep her share of the world record with gold medallist Jean Shirley.

Shortly after the Olympics Mildred was deemed to be a sporting professional after she appeared in an advertisement. She spent a time in Vaudeville before turning her attentions to her next sport – golf. Typically, she became an outstanding competitor at that as well. In one remarkable spell from 1946 to 1947 she won 14 straight tournaments, and in 1947 she became the first American winner of the British Amateur Championship. She turned professional the following year and proceeded to win the US Women's Open, and for the first four years of the US Ladies' Tour (1948–51) she was top money winner each year. She won a second Open by nine strokes in 1950.

Tragedy struck Mildred in 1953 when she had to undergo surgery for cancer, but less than 18 months later she captured the US Women's Open for a third time, when she won by a staggering 12 strokes. However, the cancer returned and the girl voted 'Athlete of the Half Century' by the US Media lost her last battle in 1956.

Zaharias with the 1954 US Open trophy.

THE GREAT GOLFERS

Mildred Zaharias

Born Port Arthur, Texas, 1914. A great all-round sportswoman, she enjoyed a successful amateur golfing career before turning professional. US Amateur Champion in 1946 she went on to win the US Women's Open three times in 1948, 1950 and 1954. Died 1956.

In 1947 Zaharias became the first American winner of the British Open Amateur Championship.

Zaharias at the 1932 Olympics.

MICKEY WRIGHT

Mickey Wright stands second only to the great Kathy Whitworth as the most successful lady golfer in the United States. Her total of 82 Tour wins is just six behind Whitworth's tally.

During the 1960s Wright was invincible and won 44 tournaments in the four years between 1961 and 1964. Accordingly, she was the top money winner in each of these years. In 1963 she won a record 13 tournaments in a season. She also notched up a record 12

THE GREAT GOLFERS

Mickey Wright

Born San Diego, California, 1935. Wright's 82 Tour wins include a record-equalling four US Women's Opens – 1958, 1959, 1961 and 1964 – and four LPGA Championship victories – 1958, 1960, 1961 and 1963.

In the early 1960s Mickey Wright was invincible. Her total of 82 US Tour wins is second only to Kathy Whitworth's tally.

Mickey Wright, one of the most successful woman golfers of all time.

women's Majors winning the US Women's Open four times. When she first won in 1958, aged 23, she was the youngest ever winner that same year she did the double by winning the US LPGA Championship, a title she won three more times. She was also twice winner of both the Western Open and Titleholders Championship. These two Majors are no longer in existence.

KATHY WHITWORTH

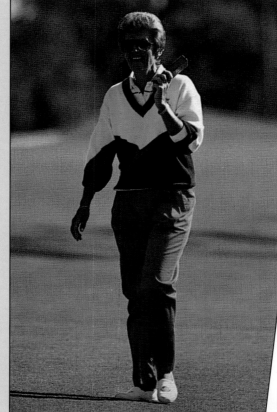

Kathy Whitworth has been to the ladies' game what Sam Snead was to the men's game. Both won more tournaments than any other professional, though Whitworth's tally of 88 is seven better than 'Slammin' Sam's. Remarkably, both players also share an unwanted distinction: despite their grand total of tournament wins, neither won their respective US Open titles. The nearest Kathy came was in 1971 when she finished second, seven shots behind JoAnne Carner.

Between 1965 and 1973 she was the top money winner eight times in nine years, during which time she won 61 of her 88 tournaments, including five of her six Majors, the first being the 1965 Titleholders Championship. She reached the record of the most women's titles in 1982 and the following year became the first woman to win $1 million.

THE GREAT GOLFERS

Kathy Whitworth

Born Monahans, Texas, 1939. With more than 88 successes on the US Tour Kathy Whitworth has won more golf tournaments than any other lady golfer. In fact she is the most prolific golfer – male or female – in the history of the game.

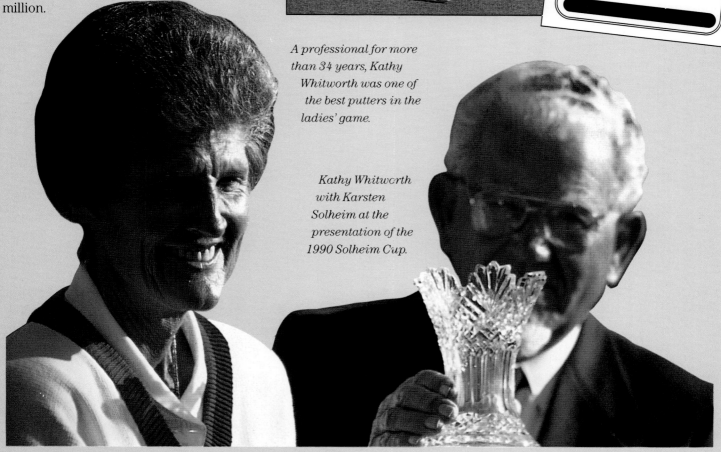

A professional for more than 34 years, Kathy Whitworth was one of the best putters in the ladies' game.

Kathy Whitworth with Karsten Solheim at the presentation of the 1990 Solheim Cup.

PAT BRADLEY

A golfer since the age of 11, Pat Bradley went on to become the biggest earner in women's golf. She turned professional in 1974 at the age of 23. Two years later she won her first Tour event when she took the Girl Talk Classic.

Bradley won her first Major, the Peter Jackson Classic in 1980 and the following year she captured the US Women's Open after one of the best head-to-heads the ladies' game has ever seen. Pat and Beth Daniel had drawn level at the 6th hole in the final round at La Grange, Illinois, and they then matched each other shot-for-shot over the next nine holes until Pat sunk a monster 75-foot putt at the 16th to swing the advantage her way. She held on to take the title with a championship record of 291 strokes.

The 1980 Championship remains Pat's only US Women's Open win but she has won six Majors including the US LPGA, Nabisco Dinah Shore and Du Maurier, all in 1986. This was a memorable year for Pat in which she won five tournaments, took home nearly $½ million in prize-money, and became the first person to surpass $2 million in winnings. She has since taken her earnings to $4.3 million and is the most successful lady golfer of all time.

Pat Bradley at the 1990 Solheim Cup, Lake Nona.

Pat Bradley

THE GREAT GOLFERS

Pat Bradley

Born Westford, Massachusetts, 1951. During her career Bradley has won six majors – the Peter Jackson Classic, the US Women's Open, the US LPGA Championship, the Nabisco Dinah Shore and the Du Maurier Classic twice.

NANCY LOPEZ

After an outstanding amateur career, Nancy Lopez turned professional in 1977 and immediately made an impact when she finished second in the US Open at Hazeltine, scene of Tony Jacklin's 1970 US Open triumph. Remarkably, it was Nancy's first tournament as a professional.

Nancy's first full season was in 1978, and what a season it was. She won her first Tour event, the Bent Tree Ladies' Classic and went on to win a further eight events, five in succession which included the US LPGA Championship. Her winnings of $189,000 were a record and she was both Player and Rookie of the Year. She was top money winner again in 1979.

Surprisingly, flaws developed in Lopez's game in 1980. A hook appeared and her putting, which had been one of her best points, started letting her down. She also had marital problems. However, she overcame these setbacks and returned to winning ways until she took a couple of 'times out' to have two children after her marriage to New York Mets baseball player Ray Knight.

In between the two new arrivals to the Lopez household, she managed to add a second US LPGA title to her name in 1985, and in 1989 she won it for a third time. Her career earnings of $3.5 million put her fifth on the all-time career money-winning list.

THE GREAT GOLFERS

Nancy Lopez

Born Torrance, California, 1957. Lopez is one of the top money winners in ladies golf even though she has only won three Majors. She is also immensely popular and she has done much to promote women's golf.

The awesome power of Nancy Lopez.

Getting out of the rough doesn't seem to pose any problems at the 1978 Colgate Tournament.

ANNIKA SORENSTAM

THE GREAT GOLFERS

Annika Sorenstam

Born in Stockholm, Sweden in October 1970.
Annika Sorenstam is considered by many experts to be the best-ever female golfer. She combines a cool efficiency with a passionate desire to win. She is among the longest hitters on the LPGA tour while also being among the most accurate.

Annika was a member of the Swedish National Team for five years, which culminated in 1992 when she won the World Amateur Championship and was also runner-up at the US Women's Amateur. In 1993 Annika was awarded Rookie of the Year award on the Ladies European Tour and in 1994 joined the LPGÁ Team. Sorenstam later went on to win her first major professional, the US Women's Open, in 1995 and 1996. Since then Annika has collected more awards and won more titles than any other LPGA player apart from Kathy Whitworth.

She set 30 LPGA records in winning eight tournaments, then in 2002 became only the second LPGA player to win 11 tournaments in a year. She played the Men's PGA tour's Colonial tournament in 2003 narrowly missing the cut. Annika won the Kraft Nabisco in 2005, 2002 and 2003. The McDonald's LPGA Championship in 2003 and 2004 and the Weetabix Women's British Open in 2003.

She became the first LPGA player ever to win more than US$ 2 million in a single season. Her career-low round is a magical 59 during the 2001 LPGA Standard Register tournament.

Annika Sorenstam has a very high level of fitness and has very strong arms with well developed forearms. This allows her to keep close control of the golf ball and enables her to compete with men over 18 holes.

THE GREAT TOURNAMENTS

Although golf matches and tournaments have been played for more than 200 years, championship golf as we know it today started in October 1860 with the first British Open at Prestwick, in Scotland. Since that memorable day, many more championships have been inaugurated.

Below, Colin Montgomerie wins the 2004 Ryder Cup for the European team at Oakland Hills, USA.

THE MAJORS

The British Open, US Open, US Professional Golfers Championship (US PGA) and the Masters are the four major championships which are played each year. Although they are collectively referred to as the Grand Slam, no one has ever won all the titles in the same year, and only four players – Gene Sarazen, Ben Hogan, Jack Nicklaus and Gary Player – have won them all.

THE BRITISH OPEN

It all started on Wednesday 17 October 1860 when eight top golfers gathered at Scotland's Prestwick links to play three rounds of the 12-hole course. All entrants, with the exception of George Brown from Blackheath, London, were members of Scottish clubs and the honour of becoming the first Open champion fell to Musselburgh's Willie Park. He beat off a challenge from Old Tom Morris by two strokes with a winning score of 174 for the 36 holes.

A painting of the Open champions at St Andrews by Michael Brown.

Willie Park Senior just after he had won the first British Open, 1860.

Morris won the second title and became the first great champion, winning the Open four times between 1861 and 1867. He was succeeded by his son, Young Tommy, who won four successive titles between 1868 and 1872. There was no tournament in 1871 because Young Tom was allowed to keep the trophy, the red Moroccan Belt, after his third successive win in 1870. When he won his fourth title, he was presented with the silver claret jug which remains one of the most cherished trophies in world golf.

Sadly, Young Tom Morris died at an early age but there were plenty of aspirants ready to challenge for the game's senior trophy, and Jamie Anderson (1877–79) and Bob Ferguson (1880–82) both won three successive titles. It would be 70 years before that feat was emulated.

Prestwick staged each of the first 12 championships, but by the turn of the century, St Andrews, Musselburgh, Muirfield, Sandwich and Hoylake had all hosted the championship. Along with the new courses came new champions, but the success of Taylor at Sandwich in 1894 heralded the start of a new era in Open Championship golf.

One of the 'Great Triumvirate', along with James Braid and Harry Vardon, Taylor and his colleagues dominated the event and won it 16 times between them in the 21 years from 1894 to 1914.

After World War I the Americans had their first breakthrough when Jock Hutchison, an exiled Briton, took the trophy across the Atlantic for the first time in 1921. A year later the flamboyant Hagen became the first American-born winner. The British domination was over and, apart from the occasional victory, they have never really regained it.

The 1920s and early part of the 1930s certainly belonged to American golfers and with the arrival of amateur Bobby Jones, British fans were privileged to witness one of the finest golfers ever seen, amateur or professional. He won the Open in 1926 and 1927 and in 1930 he beat American professionals Leo Diegel and Macdonald Smith by two strokes to capture his third title. Significantly, it was one of the four legs of an amazing Grand Slam which saw Jones win the British and US Opens, and British and US Amateur titles in one year.

Britons regained their domination in the latter half of the 1930s with the first of Cotton's three triumphs in 1934. He was the last Briton before Faldo to win three titles.

It looked as though the swing would return to the Americans after Sam Snead won at St Andrews in 1946 but victories for Fred Daly and Henry Cotton, brought about renewed optimism for the British. But it was short-lived because the next 12 years saw the British Open dominated by South African and Australian golfers.

South Africa's Bobby Locke and Australia's Peter Thomson shared nine titles between them, with Thomson achieving a post-war record of five titles, his last coming in 1965. Gary Player (South Africa) and Kel Nagle (Australia) also lent their hand to the 'Commonwealth Invasion'.

American golfers had, by the end of the 1950s, started to shun the Championship, and the number of professionals making the journey across the Atlantic each year was gradually declining. But Arnold Palmer changed all that. He came to Royal Birkdale

Walter Hagen recovers from the sand in the 1929 British Open.

Palmer during his first British Open. His presence was an inspiration for future American golfers.

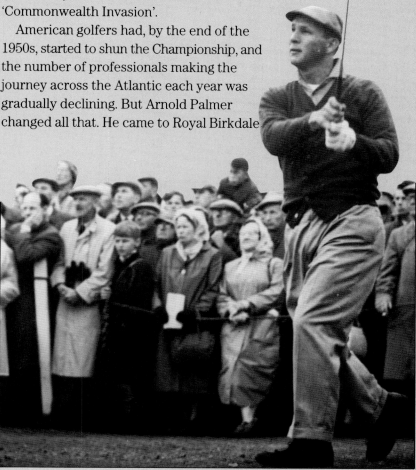

The British Open at St Andrews, 1990, where Nick Faldo was the Champion.

The early promise of Seve Ballesteros was realized in 1979 when he captured his first British Open title.

in 1961 with a new air of enthusiasm, and carried off the title. He retained it at Troon a year later, but more importantly, he made sure his fellow Americans made the annual trip, thus preventing the Open from losing its status as the world's top tournament.

Palmer's arrival also heralded the start of golf's next 'Triumvirate' – Palmer, Jack Nicklaus and Gary Player. They won the Open eight times between them, but were also the inspiration of many future champions.

American golfers once again started to dominate the event in the 1960s though there was a rare moment of delight for the British fans when Tony Jacklin became the first home champion for 18 years, after beating the New Zealander Bob Charles at Royal Lytham and St Anne's in 1969.

This was, however, to be Britain's last piece of glory until Sandy Lyle's triumph at Sandwich 16 years later. In the meantime, all eyes switched to America's Tom Watson who

won his first title after a play-off with Jack Newton at Carnoustie in 1975. That was the first of five wins including his remarkable triumph by one stroke over Jack Nicklaus at Turnberry in 1977.

In 1979 Severiano Ballesteros won the first of his three titles at Lytham. Ballesteros won the title for a second time in 1984 bringing about the end of the American supremacy. Between 1984 and 1995 the trophy only went to America once when Mark Calcavecchia was the surprise winner at Troon in 1989.

The 1980s and early 1990s really belonged to Britain. Sandy Lyle started the winning streak at Sandwich in 1985, and then Nick Faldo won three titles in 1987, 1990 and 1992 to become the first Briton since Henry Cotton to achieve a hat-trick of wins.

Greg Norman won twice in 1986 and 1993 and Ian Baker-Finch won in 1991. Nick Price won in 1994 and since then Americans have dominated the world's best-known golfing trophy: John Daly 1995, Tom Lehman 1996, Justin Leonard 1997 and Mark O'Meara at Royal Birkdale in 1998.

In 1999 Scotsman Paul Lawrie won at a stormy Carnoustie after a four way play off. In 2000, Tiger Woods won his first title, followed by David Duval in 2001 and Ernie Els in 2002. The 2003 and 2004 were won by Americans Ben Curtis and Todd Hamilton.

In 2005 Tiger Woods, after leading from the start, won his second Open by four shots from Colin Montgomerie at St Andrews, Scotland.

Above, Woods loses his ball on the first hole of the first round at The 2003 Open at Sandwich.

Left, Woods wins his second Open at St Andrews 2005.

The British Open

First played at Prestwick, Scotland, in October 1860, the British Open is now played on links courses throughout Britain annually. Vardon holds the record of six wins and Watson the lowest winning score of 268.

THE US OPEN

After the British Open the US Open is the second oldest of the four Majors, having been first played at Newport, Rhode Island, on 4 October 1895. Eleven men gathered at Newport to do battle against the 9-hole course and at the end of four rounds the winner was English-born Horace Rawlins with a score of 173.

Expatriates dominated the early championships and in 1900 Britain's leading player, Harry Vardon, made the trip across the Atlantic. In capturing the title he attracted a great deal of attention, with his unique style of play, and helped popularize the game in America. He did what Palmer did for the British Open in the 1960s.

The first 16 Opens were all won by British-born golfers but Johnny McDermott became the first American-born winner in 1911, retaining his title the following year. When the unknown amateur, Francis Ouimet, won

Left: Francis Ouimet, the surprise winner of the 1913 US Open. His victory changed the shape of world golf.

at Brookline in 1913 he beat Vardon and another talented Briton, Ted Ray, in a three-way play-off, and confirmed the end of British domination. Tony Jacklin's win at Hazeltine in 1970 has been the only British success since then.

Most of the great names of American golf have captured the US Open. Bobby Jones, Ben Hogan, Willie Anderson and Jack

Nicklaus have all won it a record four times. But one man whose name was never inscribed on the trophy was the great Sam Snead, even though he finished second four times.

Walter Hagen won his first Major when he captured the Open at only his second attempt in 1914. Hagen's great rival of the 1920s, Gene Sarazen, took his first Major in 1922 when he beat John Black and Bobby Jones to win the Open at Skokie, Illinois.

Some of the great names of modern golf have added their names to the famous trophy. Johnny Miller, Hale Irwin, Jerry Pate and Hubert Green all won in the 1970s as a new generation of American golfer was emerging. And in the 1980s it was Larry Nelson, Fuzzy Zoeller and Curtis Strange who captured the top prize in American golf. The one man who looked like going through his career without winning a Major was Tom Kite, but he rectified the situation in 1992 when he won the US Open.

In the past few years the winners have been Tiger Woods both in 2000 and 2002. Retief Goosen won in 2001 and 2004. Jim Furyk won in 2003 and the New Zealander Michael Campbell won unexpectedly in 2005.

Far left, Still in discomfort from his accident the previous year, Ben Hogan miraculously went on to win the US Open in 1950.

Below, Tony Jacklin receiving the trophy after becoming the first British winner of the US Open for 50 years at the monster Hazeltine course in 1970.

Two of the greatest names in world golf, Arnold Palmer (left) and Jack Nicklaus (right). They are seen here during the play-off for the 1967 US Open.

THE GREAT TOURNAMENTS

The US Open

First played at Newport, Rhode Island, in 1895, the US Open is now played on a different course each year in July. Anderson, Jones, Hogan and Nicklaus have each won this Major four times, and Nicklaus holds the lowest winning score of 272.

The Open has seen many great moments, but for sheer brilliance Ben Hogan's triumph at Merion in 1950 will never be surpassed. Having survived a head-on car crash in 1949 when Hogan was told he would probably never walk again, let alone play golf, he made a remarkable comeback and defied all the medics to take his second Open championship just 18 months later. Many thought Hogan would not be able to last the gruelling pace of four rounds. He did, and at the end of 72 holes was tied with George Fazio and Lloyd Mangrum on 287. An 18-hole play-off was required and Hogan beat the other two, and the many sceptics, by four and six strokes respectively for a tremendous, and emotional, win.

For the ups and downs of the Open, Arnold Palmer will probably not need reminding about how he threw away the 1966 Championship at the Olympic Club, California. After three rounds Palmer led Billy Casper by three strokes. With nine holes left to play he had increased his lead over Casper to seven strokes. Victory seemed assured – but nothing is certain in golf until the last putt is sunk. Casper gained shots at

the 10th and 13th, but Palmer met with disaster at the par 3 15th after he two-putted for a four while Casper made a birdie. Suddenly the lead was down to three. Then the lead was cut to one after the next hole when Casper made a birdie four to Palmer's bogey six at the 604-yard par 5 after a wayward tee shot.

A five to Casper's par 4 at 17 meant they were all square going into the 18th. Both men made par at the last and so a play-off was required. Palmer trailed by two after nine holes and ran out losing by four shots. But that is golf, and it is stories such as this which help make tournaments like the US Open as great as they are.

THE MASTERS

The Masters is one of the most coveted prizes in golf despite the fact that it is the youngest of the four Majors.

The Masters and the Augusta National course over which it is played were both the brainchild of Augusta-born Bobby Jones, one of the greatest amateur golfers of all time.

Jones wanted a course of beauty and this objective was achieved thanks to top designer Alister Mackenzie. Sadly, the first Masters in 1934 did not arouse the interest Jones had hoped, and in an effort to attract media attention he came out of retirement. Horton Smith snatched victory from Craig Wood with a birdie and par at the 71st and 72nd holes to take the title by one stroke.

The following year Wood was runner-up again, after losing a play-off to Gene Sarazen, who played one of the most memorable shots in golf, even to this day. Sarazen was trailing Wood by three strokes when he came to the par 5 15th in the final round. After a good drive, he took a 4-wood and holed his shot from 220 yards for an albatross (double eagle) two. Three pars then assured him of a place in the play-off and ultimate victory.

Ben Hogan and Sam Snead dominated the event in the early post-war years, winning five titles in six years between 1949 and 1954.

Horton Smith, winner of the first Masters in 1934 when he snatched victory by one stroke from Craig Wood thanks to a birdie at the 71st and par at the last hole.

A collection of official Masters badges.

They were followed by Arnold Palmer and Jack Nicklaus who between them dominated the event in the late 1950s and 1960s.

Nicklaus seemed to make the Masters his own event, and his record of six wins is two more than Palmer's next-best total. Nicklaus first won by one stroke from Tony Lema in 1963 but his second title in 1965 was by nine strokes from his great rivals Palmer and Gary Player. He became the first man to win back-to-back titles in 1966 when he won a three-way play-off with Tommy Jacobs and Gay Brewer. Triumph number four was in 1972, and in 1975 he held off a challenge from Johnny Miller and Tom Weiskopf to win by one stroke in what has been described as the best Masters of them all.

After achieving five wins, Nicklaus won himself his sixth coveted victor's green jacket in 1986, becoming the oldest Masters' champion at the age of 46 when he pipped Tom Kite and Greg Norman by one stroke for a remarkable win.

European golfers have been very successful at winning the Masters starting when Severiano Ballesteros became the Masters champion in 1980, followed by Bernhard Langer in 1985. Sandy Lyle became the first British champion in 1988. Nick Faldo won back to back titles in 1989 and 1990 followed by Ian Woosnam in 1991 making it four British wins on the spin. Bernhard Langer won again in 1993, Jose-Maria Olazabal in 1994 and Nick Faldo won his third title in 1996. Olazabal won again in 1999.

Tiger Woods has recently been the most successful winner of the Masters. In 1997, when only 21, he celebrated his first victory. Then he won back to back titles in 2001 and 2002 and completed a fourth success by winning in 2005.

Right, Tiger Woods holed directly from the bunker with this shot on the 16th green at the 2005 Masters which he went on to win after a play off with Chris Dimarco

THE GREAT TOURNAMENTS

The Masters

Played annually at the Augusta National Club, Georgia, the Masters was founded by Bobby Jones in 1934. Jack Nicklaus has won the title a record six times. Tiger Woods has won 4 times and holds the lowest winning round score of 270.

The Masters champion 2005, Tiger Woods receives the Green Jacket from the previous winner, Phil Mickelson.

UNITED STATES PGA
CHAMPIONSHIP

Although it is one of golf's four Majors, the US PGA Championship receives less publicity worldwide than the other three, largely because entry is based on performances in the United States. Consequently there have been fewer non-American winners. Among them Gary Player of South Africa in 1962 and 1972, the Australians David Graham and Wayne Grady in 1979 and 1990 and Nick Price in 1992 and 1994. Other winners are: Steve Elkington 1995, Mark Brooks 1996, Davis Love III 1997, Vijay Singh 1998, Tiger Woods 1999 and 2000, David Toms 2001, Rich Beem 2002, Shaun Micheel 2003. Vijay Singh won for a second time in 2004, and USA's Phil Mickelson became champion in 2005.

Traditionally the last of the four Majors each year, the first PGA Championship was held at Siwanoy, New York, in 1916. Jim Barnes, an Englishman living in America won the final by one hole. The event was played under match-play conditions until 1958. It was during its match-play days that the Championship brought out the best in Walter Hagen, who won five titles in seven years between 1921 and 1927. Jack Nicklaus has since equalled Hagen's record of five wins. Gene Sarazen and Sam Snead have three wins each. In the match-play days, the greatest final was in 1930 when the American Tommy Armour beat Gene Sarazen. On the last, Tommy Armour holed a putt from 14 feet. Gene Sarazen then played a similar putt to stay level but missed by inches and thus threw away the chance of his third title.

English-born Jim Barnes (putting) was the first US PGA champion in 1916 beating Scottish-born Jock Hutchison by one hole.

Vijay Singh has won the US PGA twice – 1998 and 2004.

THE GREAT TOURNAMENTS

The US PGA

First held in 1916 at Siwanoy, New York, the US PGA is now played throughout the USA every August. Hagen and Nicklaus have each won this Major five times and Bobby Nichols holds the lowest winning score of 271.

THE TEAM TOURNAMENTS

Samuel Ryder (right) with his good friend Abe Mitchell. It is said that the statue on top of the Ryder Cup is modelled on Mitchell.

Abe Mitchell   Samuel Ryder

Programmes from the two Ryder Cup matches played at the Southport and Ainsdale links in Lancashire, England. Britain won in 1933, but the Americans got their revenge four years later.

THE RYDER CUP

When it comes to team tournaments there is none greater than the Ryder Cup, a biennial match between professional golfers from the United States and Europe.

It is named after a British seed merchant, Samuel Ryder, who left his father's business in Sale, Cheshire, to set up on his own at St Albans, Hertfordshire, in the late nineteenth century. However, overwork brought about a decline in Ryder's health and at the suggestion of a local minister, Reverend Frank Wheeler, Ryder joined the local Verulam Golf Club. Suddenly, golf became the new 'love' of his life.

He was captain of the club three times and he enticed many of the leading professionals of the day to compete in tournaments at the Verulam, including the 'Great Triumvirate' of Braid, Taylor and Vardon. A great friend of Ryder's was professional Abe Mitchell, and it was probably at his suggestion that Ryder set up the Ryder Cup.

The golfer depicted on the lid of the Ryder Cup trophy is modelled on Mitchell.

The idea for a regular match came after the professionals of Britain and the United States met in a match at Wentworth in 1926; the British team won by 13½–1½.

Twelve months later, on 3 and 4 June 1927, two eight-man teams from America and Great Britain met at Worcester, Massachusetts, with Walter Hagen and Ted Ray as the respective captains of the first official Ryder Cup teams.

RYDER CUP OFFICIAL SOUVENIR PROGRAMME

PRICE 1/-

THE FOURTH INTERNATIONAL GOLF MATCH
GREAT BRITAIN *versus* THE UNITED STATES OF AMERICA
TO BE PLAYED ON THE SOUTHPORT AND AINSDALE COURSE, SOUTHPORT
ON MONDAY AND TUESDAY, JUNE 26-27, 1933.

RYDER CUP OFFICIAL SOUVENIR PROGRAMME

TO BE PLAYED TUESDAY AND WEDNESDAY, JUNE 29-30, 1937.

ON THE SOUTHPORT AND AINSDALE COURSE, SOUTHPORT, LANCS.

THE SIXTH INTERNATIONAL GOLF MATCH
GREAT BRITAIN *versus* THE UNITED STATES OF AMERICA

PRICE ONE SHILLING

America won the first match 9½–2½, but two years later when it was held on British soil, at Moortown, Leeds, Britain gained revenge when George Duncan led the British team to victory by 7–5. The Americans won on home soil again two years later and Britain levelled the series at 2-all after a narrow 6½–5½ win at Southport and Ainsdale in 1933. But that was to be Britain's last success for 24 years as the Americans dominated Sam Ryder's tournament.

The trophy went across the Atlantic in the two remaining pre-war tournaments and when it was revived at Pinehurst in 1947 it was a repeat performance with the Americans winning 11–1. It was closer at Ganton two years later, but it was not until 1957 that the team from Great Britain, led by Dai Rees, recaptured the title at Lindrick, near Sheffield. But that was to be the last

time that a British team would win the Ryder Cup because the Americans re-took command, and in fact by the 1970s such was their dominance of the event that interest started to decline.

The addition of Irish players to the British squad in 1973 did little to lift the hopes of the team as they still suffered some heavy defeats. In 1979, in the hope of making the contest closer, the make-up of the 'British' team was changed and players from the whole of Europe became eligible for selection.

Spaniards Antonio Garrido and Severiano Ballesteros became the first players from other European countries to join the British team which opposed the Americans at Greenbrier, West Virginia, in 1979, but their presence did little to change matters and the Americans won 17–11. It was a similar story at Walton Heath, Surrey, in 1981 but two

Sam Snead served his country in nine Ryder Cup matches; the most by an American.

Dai Rees (front centre) with the British team.

years later, after the appointment of Tony Jacklin as Europe's captain, the tournament started to take on a different complexion.

At the PGA National in Florida in 1983 Jacklin's men pushed the hosts all the way before losing by one point. But two years later on home soil at The Belfry, the Europeans recorded a memorable win and thus inflicted the first defeat on the Americans since 1957.

That was not only the start of a great run of success for the European team, it was also the start of a great hype which resulted in the Ryder Cup receiving unprecedented publicity and media coverage. In 1987 Jacklin's men made more history when they travelled to Jack Nicklaus's Muirfield Village

Right, The victorious European Ryder Cup team of 2006, led by Ian Woosnam, celebrate retaining the famous trophy at the K Club, Ireland.

Right, A proud moment for Captain Ian Woosnam with the 2006 Ryder Cup.

THE GREAT TOURNAMENTS

The Ryder Cup

This famous tournament is played alternately in the USA and Britain. Founded by Sam Ryder, it was first played in Worcester Massachusetts in 1927. It is now played biennially in September between teams from Europe and the USA.

Course at Columbus, Ohio and won for the first time in America.

Europe retained the trophy at The Belfry in 1989 and had further wins in 1995 and 1997. America won at Brookline in Boston in 1999, but the Europeans had stunning victories in 2002 under Sam Torrance's captaincy and again in 2004 under captain Bernhard Langer. A third consecutive European win was in 2006 celebrated under the captaining of Ian Woosnam.

The Ryder Cup is now always keenly awaited as it has become the top international team event in world golf.

THE WALKER CUP

The Walker Cup is the amateur's equivalent of the Ryder Cup, and it predates its professional counterpart by five years.

The British team suffered some heavy defeats prior to World War II. They were trounced 11–1 at Chicago in 1928 and 10–2 at Sandwich two years later. They did not enjoy their first win until 1938, the last pre-war Walker Cup when they won 71/2–41/2 at St Andrews.

In post-war years the Americans won the Walker Cup every two years, until a draw in 1965 gave some hope to the British team. Britain's second victory did not come until 1971 when Michael Bonnallack led the team to victory. In 1989, the British team captured the Walker Cup a third time. The US regained the trophy in 1991 and retained it in 1993. The British team won in 1995 and the US won in 1997. The Great Britain and Ireland team regained the trophy in 1999 and retained it for successive wins in 2001 and 2003.

The Walker Cup

First held in 1922 the Walker Cup is a biennial competition between amateur golfers of the United States and Great Britain and Ireland. Like its professional counterpart, the Ryder Cup, it is always eagerly awaited every two years.

Below, The legendary British Walker Cup winning team of 1971 led by Michael Bonallack.

The idea of an international team tournament, not just between Britain and the USA, was first put forward in 1920 by Herbert Walker, President of the United States Golf Association. An invitation was sent to various countries but there was little or no response. However, Walker was still keen to send a team to Hoylake the following year and a challenge match between America and Britain was to be played for the International Challenge Trophy. The local press dubbed it the 'Walker Cup'. This was the first unofficial match and the United States won 9–3.

The first official Walker Cup was played a year later at Long Island, New York, and the Americans won again, this time 8–4. It was contested annually until 1924, but it then became a biennial event. No matter how often it was played, the Americans still managed to win, thanks largely to the great Bobby Jones, a player who stood head and shoulders above the rest.

THE CURTIS CUP

The ladies' equivalent of the Walker Cup is the Curtis Cup, named after sisters Harriot and Margaret Curtis who represented the United States in an international match against Great Britain at Cromer, Norfolk, in 1905; the British women won 6–1.

After several years of unofficial matches the Curtis sisters donated a trophy for a biennial match between the two countries, starting in 1932, and the United States Golf Association and the Ladies Golf Union agreed to share the organizational responsibilities. The first match was played at Wentworth, Surrey and was won by the United States 5½–3½.

America won at Chevy Chase two years later but Britain managed a draw at Gleneagles in 1936 when Jessie Anderson holed a 20 foot putt on the last green to win her match and force the tie. It was a memorable moment.

After early US domination, the British team enjoyed some success in the 1950s winning at Muirfield in 1952 and Sandwich in 1956. Furthermore, they forced a great draw at Brae Burn, Massachusetts, in 1958.

But that was the end of the British success for nearly 30 years until enjoying back-to-back wins at Prarie Dunes, Kansas in 1986 and at Sandwich two years later. The American women regained the trophy with a vengeance in 1990 with a very convincing 14–4 win, but the British team re-stamped their authority with a 10–8 win at Hoylake in 1992. Britain and Ireland retained the trophy in 1994 and won again in 1996 at Killarney. The United States won the 2004 event, extending its overall lead to 24 wins to 6, with 3 ties. Fourteen year old Michelle Wie played for the US becoming the youngest player in Curtis Cup history. She won both of her singles matches.

THE EISENHOWER TROPHY

First held in 1958, the Eisenhower Trophy is similar in conception to the idea first put

---

THE GREAT TOURNAMENTS

The Curtis Cup

Named after the American sisters Harriot and Margaret Curtis, the Curtis Cup is a team competition between women golfers of the United States and Great Britain and Ireland. It has been dominated by the Americans.

The moment of victory for the British team at Hoylake in 1992.

American President Dwight D. Eisenhower (left) was a great golfing fan. He is seen here having a laugh with Arnold Palmer.

Below, The 1980 US Amateur Champion Hal Sutton was a consistent winner on the US Tour and an individual title winner of the Eisenhower Cup before becoming US Ryder Cup Captain in 2004.

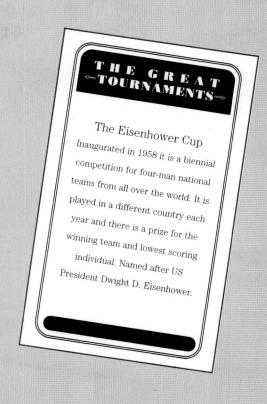

THE GREAT TOURNAMENTS

The Eisenhower Cup

Inaugurated in 1958 it is a biennial competition for four-man national teams from all over the world. It is played in a different country each year and there is a prize for the winning team and lowest scoring individual. Named after US President Dwight D. Eisenhower.

forward by George Walker back in 1920. It is an international team competition for teams of four players. The trophy is named after the former US President, Dwight D. Eisenhower, who was himself a keen golfer.

The first Eisenhower Trophy was contested at St Andrews in October 1958 and won by Australia who beat the United States in a play-off. The individual prize for the lowest aggregate score was shared by Bruce Devlin (Australia), Reid Jack (Scotland) and Bill Hyndman (USA). The winner of the second individual title at Merion two years later was Jack Nicklaus, who was also a member of the winning American team. Jerry Pate and Hal Sutton are two other well-known American professionals to have won the individual title. America, Australia and Great Britain and Ireland won the first 13 competitions between them, but the 1990s saw victories for Sweden in 1990, New Zealand in 1992, Australia 1996 and Great Britain in 1998. The Americans do however still hold the record of twelve wins in this event having won in 2000, 2002 and 2004.

AMATEUR CHAMPIONSHIPS

THE BRITISH AMATEUR CHAMPIONSHIP

The idea for this tournament was first conceived in 1878 but the Royal and Ancient showed little interest in setting up such a competition and the idea was dropped. However, in 1885, Thomas Owen Potter of Hoylake organized a competition over his home links at Royal Liverpool to find the champion amateur golfer of Britain and that honour fell to Allan McFie, a Scottish member of the host club, who beat Horace Hutchinson 7 & 6 in the final.

The following year the championship gained recognition by the Royal and Ancient who took over the organization of the event and the second championship was won by the inaugural year's runner-up, Hutchinson.

It has been a match-play competition since its formation, but in the 1980s a medal competition was introduced to reduce the field to 64 before changing to match-play conditions.

John Ball, himself a member of the Royal Liverpool Club, won the title a record eight times between 1888 and 1912 and is one of three men, along with Harold Hilton and Bobby Jones, to win both the British Amateur and British Open titles. Jones, of course, won his in the same year, 1930.

British Amateur Championship

First held at Hoylake, England in 1885 it is now the most prestigious non-professional tournament in Britain and attracts a large overseas entry each year. It is played on a different golf course each summer.

John Ball bunkered. One of the finest amateur golfers, Ball, won the British Amateur Championship a record eight times.

The biggest winning margin in any final was achieved by America's Lawson Little who beat Britain's Jack Wallace 14 & 13 in the 1934 final at Prestwick. The same year, Little won the US Amateur title by 8 & 7.

Some famous golfers have had their names engraved on the trophy over the years but only one has managed to win it three years in succession. And that was achieved by Sir Michael Bonallack, between 1968 and 1970. Deane Benman was the 1959 winnner. The best known winner has been Spain's Jose-Maria Olazabal, who won the title in 1984.

THE UNITED STATES AMATEUR CHAMPIONSHIP

Following a number of unofficial championships this tournament was officially launched in 1895, ten years after its British counterpart.

It was first played at Newport, Rhode Island, over the same course and in the same week as the inaugural US Open. The first champion was Charles Macdonald from Chicago who beat C.E. Sands 12 & 11 in a one-sided final which is the biggest winning margin of victory in a match-play final in the championship.

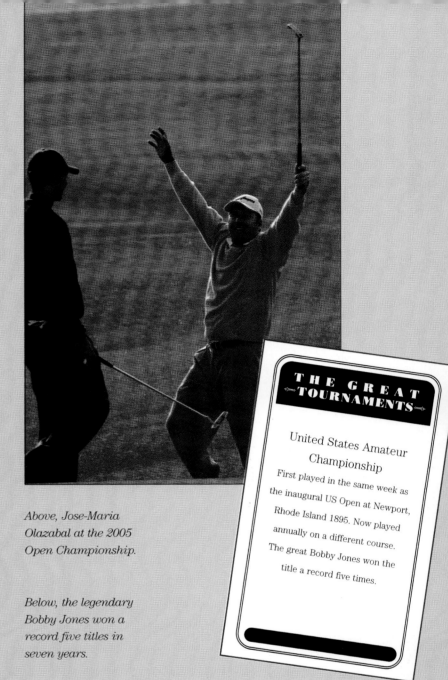

Above, Jose-Maria Olazabal at the 2005 Open Championship.

Below, the legendary Bobby Jones won a record five titles in seven years.

THE GREAT TOURNAMENTS

United States Amateur Championship

First played in the same week as the inaugural US Open at Newport, Rhode Island 1895. Now played annually on a different course. The great Bobby Jones won the title a record five times.

All championships up to 1965 were played under match-play conditions. From 1965 to 1972 it was a stroke-play event but it reverted to match-play in 1973.

The legendary Bobby Jones won a record five titles in the seven years between 1924 and 1930, his Grand Slam year. His closest win in any of the five finals by 8 & 7!

Post-war winners of the title have included some of the notable names who went on to make their mark in the professional game in the United States. The 1953 champion was Gene Littler and a year later Arnold Palmer was the Amateur Champion. Jack Nicholas won the title twice, in 1959 and 1961. Lanny Wadkins, Craig Stadler, Jerry Pate, John Cook and Mark O'Meara have all been Amateur Champions. Tiger Woods was three times US Amateur Champion in 1994, 1995 and 1996 before turning professional.

THE WOMEN'S MAJORS

US WOMEN'S OPEN CHAMPIONSHIP

Like the men, women's professional golf currently has four Majors, the oldest of which is US Women's Open, and this was launched in 1946. The first Champion was Patty Berg, one of the great lady golfers of the era. In the final she beat Betty Jameson in the only match-play tournament. All subsequent Opens have been under medal conditions. Betsy Rawls and Mickey Wright have each won the title a record four times. Patty Sheehan created a unique record in 1992 by winning both the US and British Women's Open in the same season.

McDONALD'S LPGA CHAMPIONSHIP

The LPGA Championship, currently known for sponsorship reasons as the McDonald's LPGA Championship, is the second-longest running tournament in the history of the Ladies Professional Golf Association surpassed only by the US Women's Open. It is one of the four majors on the LPGA tour. Inaugurated in 1955, five years after the formation of the US LPGA, the first winner was Beverley Hanson. Like the Open, it started life as a match-play event before becoming a medal event only one year later. Mickey Wright has been the most successful golfer in this championship with four wins, but Annika Sorenstam has won three times consecutively in 2003, 2004, 2005.

WEETABIX WOMEN'S BRITISH OPEN

The Women's British Open, also known for sponsorship reasons as the Weetabix Women's British Open, is one of the leading events in women's professional golf, being the only tournament which is classified as a major by both the Ladies European Tour and the LPGA Tour. The event was established by the Ladies Golf Union of Great Britain in 1976. It became an official stop on the LPGA Tour in 1994. It has been an LPGA major since 2001, when it took the place of the Du Maurier Classic on the list of majors.

KRAFT NABISCO CHAMPIONSHIP

The Kraft Nabisco Championship has been designated one of the LPGA Tour's majors since 1983. The tournament has actually been played however since 1972 when it was called the Colgate Dinah Shore. From 1982 to 1999 it was called the Nabisco Dinah Shore. The tournament record of 19-under par 269 was set by Dottie Pepper in 1999. It is a tradition of this championship for the winner to take a victory leap into a lake off the 18the green following her win. Annika Sorenstam has won the tournament three times in 2001, 2002 and 2005.

Right, Mickey Wright, with 82 wins on the US Tour, is the second most successful lady golfer of all time.

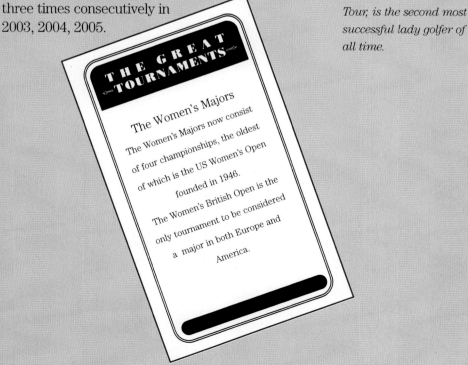

THE GREAT TOURNAMENTS

The Women's Majors

The Women's Majors now consist of four championships, the oldest of which is the US Women's Open founded in 1946. The Women's British Open is the only tournament to be considered a major in both Europe and America.

THE GOLFING TOURS

Competitive golf for professional players, both male and female, is available weekly throughout the year and is possible in all parts of the globe, thank to the various tours organized by the different golfing bodies.

The two biggest, and most popular, are those for the professional male golfers in both America and Europe, the US PGA Tour in the USA and the PGA Tour in Europe.

THE US PGA TOUR

Originally, this tour started in 1899 when the Western Open was added to the American golfing calendar to make it, along with the US Open, a two-event tour. But it was not until after the formation of the US PGA in 1916 that a tour as it is known today got under way.

It started in the 1920s when club professionals, with little work in the winter months, would gather in the warmer southern states, starting in the West and moving to the East coast before returning to their summer jobs in the clubs.

When the likes of Walter Hagen, Gene Sarazen and the amateur Bobby Jones joined the 'Tour' it gained in popularity and aided the establishment of such events as the Texas Open and the Los Angeles Open, which have remained high points of the Tour and have helped the game develop as a spectator sport.

After the war the US PGA became more of a national tour, organization improved, and when television showed an interest, prize-money increased. The effect of this is evident today as the US PGA Tour is now one of the most prestigious tours in the world.

In 1968 the professionals took control when they formed the Tournament Players' Division, and since then the Tour has gone from strength to strength.

THE PGA EUROPEAN TOUR

The PGA European Tour is Europe's equivalent of the US PGA Tour.

While European golfers have been competing against each other in the German, French, Spanish, Belgian and other Opens for many years, the Tour as we know it today started in 1971 when former Ryder Cup captain John Jacobs was appointed by the PGA to look into a way of making torurnament play for Europe's professionals a financially sound proposition.

As events increased in popularity, sponsorship grew as did the prize money. Its tournaments are mostly held in Europe, but in recent years it has expanded to other parts of the world.

In 1989 the tour visited Asia for the first time for the Dubai Desert Classic. A first visit to East

Above, Colin Montgomerie led the Order of Merit as leading money winner of the European Tour from 1993 to 1999.

THE GREAT TOURNAMENTS

Golfing Tours

The US PGA Tour is the most prestigious of the world's Tours and is followed by the European Tour. Many other Tours exist for Seniors, professionals and amateurs all around the world

Asia followed for the 1992 Johnnie Walker Classic in Bangkok.

This has since proved to be one of the most notable initiatives for the tour as East Asia has become its second home.

In 1995 the European Tour began a policy of co-sanctioning tournaments with the other PGA Tours of South Africa, Australasia and Asia. The 2005 season included five events in China, two events in South Africa and events in Singapore, Australia, New Zealand, Malaysia, Indonesia, United Arab Emirates and Qatar.

In early 2005 four of the top ten players in the World Golf Rankings were full members of the European Tour – Ernie Els, Retief Goosen, Sergio Garcia and Padraig Harrington.

THE PGA TOUR OF AUSTRALASIA

Competitive golf is now available all the year round for the leading professionals; when it is winter in America or Europe they can make their way to Oceania for the Australasian Tour. The New Zealand Open, Australian Open, Australian Masters, Australian PGA and Heineken Classic are prestigious events some of which are co-sanctioned with the European and Asian Tours. Many of the top professionals from both sides of the Atlantic make the trip down under in the hope of catching some sun, titles and cash. The quality of the Australasian Tour can be seen in the wealth of talented golfers it has produced in recent years: Greg Norman, David Graham, Adam Scott, Craig Parry, Nick O'Hearn and 2005 US Open winner Michael Campbell.

Above, The popularity of golf in Asia can be seen by the size of the crowd as Tiger Woods sizes up a putt during the Johnnie Walker Classic at Blue Canyon, Phuket, Thailand

THE ASIAN TOUR

One of the fastest growing tours in recent years, the Asian Tour started as the Far East Tour back in 1959 with the first Hong Kong Open. But since then the golf boom has exploded beyond all expectation in Asia particularly in Japan, Korea, Singapore, Thailand and China where they cannot build golf courses fast enough to satisfy demand. In recent years top American and European golfers have had stiff competiton from local golfers from Australasia. This has helped to boost the popularity of tournaments such as the Singapore Open and the Taiwan Open. Co-sanctioned events with European Tour have increased the prize money making it one of the richest tours.

THE SUNSHINE TOUR

The Sunshine Tour is the professional golf tour based in South Africa. For much of its history it was know as the South African tour, but it has rebranded itself in an attempt to broaden its appeal. However a large majority of the tour events are still staged in South Africa. The tour is one of the leading men's tours with some of the more prestigious events co-sanctioned with the PGA European Tour to attract stronger fields.

Top World Ranking golfers from South Africa Ernie Els and Retief Goosen both started their professional careers on this tour.

THE WOMEN'S TOURS

THE US LPGA TOUR

The US LPGA Tour has come a long way since its early years after the formation of the Ladies' Professional Golf Association (LPGA) in 1950. Television coverage and sponsorship has helped the growth of the tour as well as the increasing popularity of women's golf in general. The majority of the LPGA Tour's events are held in the USA, however some events are now scheduled in Mexico, and Canada. Two events are co-sanctioned with the Ladies European Tour, the Women's British Open and the Evian Masters in France. One event is held in South Korea, which now has a large contingent of players on the tour, and is co-sanctioned with the LPGA of Korea Tour. In the early decades the LPGA Tour was dominated by American players, but the non-US contingent is now very large. Annika Sorenstam of Sweden and Karrie Webb of Australia have dominated since 1997 with Sorenstam topping the money list since 2001.

THE LADIES EUROPEAN TOUR

The Ladies Euroepan Tour is the world's second ranked professional golf tour for women after the US LPGA tour. It was founded in 1979.

In 2005 there were approximately twenty events on the Tour's schedule. Most of these in Europe, but the tour also co-sanctions the ANZ Ladies Masters in Australia and includes a couple of events in Asia. In July 2005 the tour dismissed its fifth chief executive in eight years, finding it very difficult to compete effectively against the US LPGA Tour for players and media attention even within Europe.

Unlike men's golf the European and American Tours do not share a common set of majors, although the Women's British Open is recognised as a major by both Tours. The only other event recognised as a major on the European Tour is the Evian Masters played in France. The US LPGA doesn't recognise it as major but co-sanctions the event as part of its regular schedule.

Below, Annika Sorenstam has dominated the US LPGA Tour, topping the money list since 2001.

GREAT GOLF
COURSES

With the increasing popularity of the game of
golf the number of courses is growing all the
time. The courses included in this chapter have
all hosted the major tournaments, been the
scene for triumphs and disappointments, and
provided challenges to the great golfers,
challenges such as the 8th hole at Pebble Beach
where the green juts out into the Pacific.

BRITISH ISLES

THE BELFRY

Since its opening in 1977 the Belfry, near Sutton Coldfield in the West Midlands, has rapidly risen to the fore of British golf and is now one of its senior venues, as well as being the home of the PGA.

It was designed by Dave Thomas and Peter Alliss and has very close similarities to the Augusta National Course in America, with water a plentiful feature.

Thomas and Alliss transformed former potato fields and developed two courses, the Derby Course and the championship Brabazon Course. And it was over the latter that British golf witnessed one of its greatest scenes in 1985 when Tony Jacklin and his team of battlers wrested the Ryder Cup from the Americans after their 28-year dominance. And four years later the European team regained the trophy after a nail-biting draw.

The Belfry certainly has some of the beauty of Augusta about it and apart from hosting the Ryder Cup since 1985, it is the home of the English Open each year. It has also played host to the State Express Classic and Lawrence Batley Classic.

The beauty of the Belfry is captured in this picture of the 10th hole.

Opposite: Valderrama.

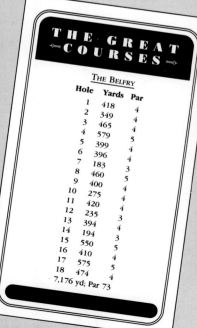

THE GREAT COURSES

THE BELFRY

Hole	Yards	Par
1	418	4
2	349	4
3	465	4
4	579	5
5	399	4
6	396	4
7	183	3
8	460	5
9	400	4
10	275	4
11	420	4
12	235	3
13	394	4
14	194	3
15	550	5
16	410	4
17	575	5
18	474	4

7,176 yd; Par 73

ROYAL BIRKDALE

One of many links courses on the Fylde coast of England, situated between Liverpool and Blackpool, Royal Birkdale is the best-known and offers the finest and most testing golf to professional and club players alike.

The club was founded in 1889 but was situated nearer to Southport town centre than the existing course, and it used the nearby Portland Hotel (still standing) as its clubhouse. They moved to their present site in 1897 and the clubhouse now stands proudly as one of the finest in England.

Birkdale received its 'Royal' status in 1951 and three years later staged its first British Open which was won by Australia's Peter Thomson. America's Arnold Palmer won the next championship to be held there in 1961. On his way to victory he played one of golf's great shots when he hit the ball from behind a bush to within 15 feet of the pin, 140 yards away at the 15th. A plaque adjacent to the bush commemorates his shot.

Thomson won his fifth post-war Open over the Southport links in 1965. Lee Trevino was Open champion at Birkdale in 1971 and in 1976 the potential of Spanish youngster Severiano Ballesteros was witnessed when he finished second to winner Johnny Miller.

Tom Watson, like Thomson, won his fifth Open at Birkdale, in 1983, and the 1991 Open champion at the famous links was Australia's Ian Baker-Finch.

The large crowd at Royal Birkdale watching Ian Baker-Finch of Australia win.

THE GREAT COURSES

ROYAL BIRKDALE			ROYAL LYTHAM		
Hole	Yards	Par	Hole	Yards	Par
1	488	4	1	206	3
2	417	4	2	437	4
3	409	4	3	457	4
4	203	3	4	393	4
5	346	4	5	212	3
6	468	4	6	490	5
7	154	3	7	549	5
8	458	4	8	394	4
9	414	4	9	164	3
10	395	4	10	334	4
11	409	4	11	542	5
12	184	3	12	198	3
13	473	4	13	342	4
14	199	3	14	445	4
15	543	5	15	463	4
16	414	4	16	357	4
17	525	5	17	462	4
18	472	4	18	412	4
6,932 yd; Par 70			6,857 yd; Par 71		

Lytham, the most northerly English course to stage the British Open.

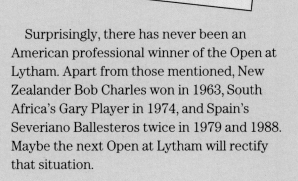

ROYAL LYTHAM

To give it its full title, the Royal Lytham and St Annes links was originally laid out in 1886 and in 1893 hosted its first championship, the British Ladies' Championship.

The club moved a short distance up the road to its present site on the Fylde Coast close to Blackpool in 1896 and in 1926 was granted 'Royal' status. That same year it hosted its first British Open, which was won by the great amateur Bobby Jones.

When the Open was next held at Lytham, 26 years later, the champion was South Africa's Bobby Locke; and his great rival of the day, Peter Thomson, won in 1958.

While it is a flat course, the wind that blows in from the sea makes Lytham as testing as any seaside course and accuracy off the tee is essential. But one man who mastered the course, and provided the British fans with a moment to remember in 1969, was Tony Jacklin who became the first home winner of the British Open for 18 years.

Surprisingly, there has never been an American professional winner of the Open at Lytham. Apart from those mentioned, New Zealander Bob Charles won in 1963, South Africa's Gary Player in 1974, and Spain's Severiano Ballesteros twice in 1979 and 1988. Maybe the next Open at Lytham will rectify that situation.

captured the title, while Player won the individual title. It is now the home of the Volvo PGA Championship, one of the leading events on the annual Volvo Tour.

CARNOUSTIE

The longest course ever to stage the British Open, Carnoustie measured 7,272 yards when it hosted its fourth Open in 1968. Even the champion, Gary Player, could not bring the giant to its knees – his winning total of 289 was the highest for 21 years.

Built at Angus in Scotland in 1842, the designers made full use of the natural terrain, and the natural hazards ensure that the closing three holes are probably the toughest in Britain, notably the par 3, 250-yard 16th, calls for nothing but the best of tee shots.

WENTWORTH

As it is not a links course, Wentworth is not eligible to host the British Open. Nevertheless, it is still one of England's best-known courses and is used for many tournaments, including the World Match-play Championship every year since its inauguration in 1964. It also hosted the Ryder Cup in 1953.

Located close to London at Virginia Water in Surrey, the original East course was opened in 1924 and the West course followed in the 1930s. At nearly 7,000 yards in length, the latter eventually became the championship course, and because of its length earned the nickname 'The Burma Road'. The par 5 17th is the longest hole at 571 yards. But to make the closing holes challenging, the 18th is also a par 5 and measures more than 500 yards.

Shortly after Wentworth opened it hosted a challenge match between the professionals of Great Britain and the United States. This was the forerunner of the Ryder Cup which was inaugurated a year later.

The other major event played at Wentworth was the Canada Cup (now the World Cup) in 1956 when Hogan and Snead

THE GREAT COURSES

WENTWORTH			CARNOUSTIE		
Hole	Yards	Par	Hole	Yards	Par
1	471	4	1	416	4
2	155	3	2	460	4
3	452	4	3	347	4
4	501	5	4	434	4
5	191	3	5	393	4
6	344	4	6	575	5
7	399	4	7	397	4
8	398	4	8	183	3
9	450	4	9	474	4
10	186	3	10	452	4
11	376	4	11	358	4
12	483	5	12	475	5
13	441	4	13	168	3
14	179	3	14	488	5
15	466	4	15	461	4
16	380	4	16	250	3
17	571	5	17	455	4
18	502	5	18	486	4
6,945 yd; Par 72			7,272 yd; Par 72		

Above: The 18th at Carnoustie.

The dog-leg 4th hole at Wentworth.

The brook, called the Barry Burn, which weaves its way across the course, comes into play at five holes and three times at the 18th.

America's Tommy Armour won Carnoustie's first Open in 1931, and in 1937 Henry Cotton won his second Open there. When Ben Hogan won in 1953 he certainly tamed the giant course. On the final day he twice birdied the par 5, 575-yard 6th hole to win by four strokes.

At Carnoustie's 1975 Open Tom Watson won his first title after a play-off against the luckless Australian Jack Newton.

The famous Gleneagles Hotel.

GLENEAGLES

The magnificent setting of the Gleneagles courses, adjacent to the famous Gleneagles Hotel, makes the Scottish course one of the most popular destinations for visitors to Scotland.

Situated at Auchterarder in Perthshire, and surrounded by the Ochils and Grampian mountains, it has one of the most beautiful settings in British golf. The Kings and Queens courses opened in 1919 and the Gleneagles Hotel five years later. The two original courses were designed by James Braid. There are now a total of four courses, all are needed to meet the demands of local and visiting golfers.

The first major individual championship held at Gleneagles was the 1935 Penfold Tournament won by Peter Allis' father, Percy. Because it is not a true links course, Gleneagles has never played host to the British Open, but its survival has not depended on hosting major championships as its beauty has ensured that it is one of the world's most visited golf courses.

THE GREAT COURSES

GLENEAGLES			MUIRFIELD		
Hole	Yards	Par	Hole	Yards	Par
1	362	4	1	449	4
2	436	4	2	349	4
3	374	4	3	379	4
4	466	4	4	181	3
5	178	3	5	558	5
6	480	5	6	471	4
7	444	4	7	185	3
8	178	3	8	444	4
9	409	4	9	495	5
10	499	5	10	475	4
11	230	3	11	386	4
12	442	4	12	381	4
13	464	4	13	153	3
14	342	4	14	447	4
15	459	4	15	396	4
16	158	3	16	188	3
17	377	4	17	542	5
18	525	5	18	447	4
6,832 yd; Par 71			6,926 yd; Par 71		

MUIRFIELD

Muirfield first hosted the British Open in 1892 when the title was won by Englishman Harold Hilton. One hundred years later, the British Open was played over the famous Scottish course again, and another Englishman, Nick Faldo, carried off the title. It was the fourteenth time that Muirfield, the home of the Honourable Company of Edinburgh Golfers, had hosted the Open.

The Honourable Company of Edinburgh Golfers is one of the oldest golf clubs and moved from Musselburgh to its new home at Muirfield in 1892. The original layout was designed by Old Tom Morris. Situated on the Firth of Forth, the course in its present-day form provides one of the sternest tests for the professional golfer. In addition to its length, nearly 7,000 yards, the winds blowing off the Forth can make conditions even more hazardous.

Severe rough is also a problem at Muirfield but these difficult conditions have provided the setting for some of the most exciting championships. Henry Cotton gave a wonderful display of driving to win the 1948 Open at Muirfield, and in 1966 Nicklaus won his first Open here. And it was after the famous Scottish course that Nicklaus named 'his' course Muirfield Village at Ohio. In 1971 Lee Trevino deprived another Briton, Tony Jacklin, of victory, when he chipped in at the 71st for victory.

Because of its location, Muirfield is a perfect course for the spectator and it is for this reason that it has staged most leading tournaments, including the 1973 Ryder Cup when the tournament was played in Scotland for the first time.

ST ANDREWS

The home of golf, the sport has been played in the Burgh of St Andrews since 1552, and possibly earlier.

The Society of St Andrews' Golfers was formed in May 1754 and is one of the world's oldest. The site of the original course is uncertain but it is known that Baillie Glass was used as the clubhouse before moving the '19th' to the Union Parlour.

In 1834 the Society changed its name to the Royal and Ancient after William IV agreed to become the club's first patron. Twenty years later, and 100 years after the Society's formation, the current clubhouse was built.

By the end of the nineteenth century, the Royal and Ancient was highly respected by other clubs and was one of the three organizers of the British Open. Its recognition grew to such an extent that it became regarded as the authority on the rules of golf. The club still holds this position today.

Situated alongside St Andrews Bay, the original course contained 22 holes but with only 11 greens. Those large, double-holed greens remain a major feature of the Old Course at St Andrews. One of the most renowned holes in British golf, the 17th, known as the Road Hole, is notorious for

An undated painting of St Andrews.

The Hell bunker at St Andrews is one *of the world's most famous bunkers.*

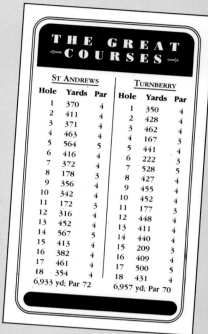

Open in 1986, when Australia's Greg Norman was champion.

The backdrop of the Ailsa Craig and Isle of Arran offers one of the finest settings in British golf, and has done since the Marquis of Ailsa laid out the first course on his private Scottish estate in the nineteenth century. The Turnberry Hotel Golf Club was established in 1903 and between the two world wars a second course was built, thus providing the Ailsa and Arran courses, the Ailsa is the championship course used today.

The course suffered extensive damage during World War II when it was seconded by the RAF Coastal Command, but thanks to the magnificent efforts of Frank Hole and Mackenzie Ross, it was restored to its former glory by 1951 and in the 1950s it hosted Scottish Championships. When it staged the *News of the World* Match-play Championship in 1957 it was hailed as a great championship course by the professionals of the day.

THE GREAT COURSES

St Andrews			Turnberry		
Hole	Yards	Par	Hole	Yards	Par
1	370	4	1	350	4
2	411	4	2	428	4
3	371	4	3	462	4
4	463	4	4	167	3
5	564	5	5	441	4
6	416	4	6	222	3
7	372	4	7	528	5
8	178	3	8	427	4
9	356	4	9	455	4
10	342	4	10	452	4
11	172	3	11	177	3
12	316	4	12	448	4
13	452	4	13	411	4
14	567	5	14	440	4
15	413	4	15	209	3
16	382	4	16	409	4
17	461	4	17	500	5
18	354	4	18	431	4
6,933 yd; Par 72			6,957 yd; Par 70		

The 4th green at Turnberry with the beautiful backdrop of Ailsa Craig.

being one of the world's most difficult holes. It has claimed many victims over the years as championship-winning rounds have come unstuck at this infamous par 4.

A second course, the New Course was constructed in 1894 and before the end of the century, the Jubilee course was completed. A fourth, the Eden course, was added in 1912. St Andrews has hosted over 20 Opens, since its first in 1873.

TURNBERRY

Turnberry had to wait a long time before staging its first British Open, but when it came, in 1977, it came with a vengeance, as Tom Watson and Jack Nicklaus shattered record after record before Watson ran out the one-stroke winner. It staged another

UNITED STATES

AUGUSTA

The Augusta National golf course offers tough demanding golf, and its setting must rank as the finest in the world.

The course was the brainchild of former champion Bobby Jones. He had a vision to design the most beautiful course in the world, fit for one of the most prestigious championships in the world – the Masters. His vision certainly became a reality as both rightly hold their place at the forefront of world golf.

Jones and his good friend Cliff Roberts recruited the services of top designer Alister Mackenzie and in 1931 the Augusta course in Georgia was opened. The plant-life is spectacular and the holes are named after the shrubs that lines each fairway. Tall pine trees and the abundance of water make Augusta even more attractive, and demanding – the lake in front of the 16th green has seen many ambitions destroyed.

The greens also offer a demanding test. The 11th, 12th and 13th holes, known as 'Amen Corner', are alongside Rae's Creek which awaits any wayward shots – something that no player can afford at Augusta.

CYPRESS POINT

While Cypress Point has never been used for a major championship, because it is only 6,506 yards long and not severe enough, it is still one of the top American courses, and one that visitors pencil in on their itinerary when touring in the California area.

Located on the Monterey Peninsula, Cypress Point is very beautiful and its lack of yards does not detract from its severity. The 16th, apart from being a much-photographed hole, demands the best of tee shots to the green 233 yards away because there is no

The 16th, like the other holes at Augusta, is picturesque. But the lake in front of the green also makes it one of the toughest.

Right: The 16th hole at Cypress Point.

THE GREAT COURSES

AUGUSTA			CYPRESS POINT		
Hole	Yards	Par	Hole	Yards	Par
1	400	4	1	418	4
2	555	5	2	551	5
3	360	4	3	161	3
4	205	3	4	385	4
5	435	4	5	491	5
6	180	3	6	522	5
7	360	4	7	163	3
8	535	5	8	355	4
9	435	4	9	291	4
10	485	4	10	491	5
11	455	4	11	434	4
12	155	3	12	409	4
13	465	5	13	362	4
14	405	4	14	383	4
15	500	5	15	139	3
16	170	3	16	233	3
17	400	4	17	376	4
18	405	4	18	342	4
6,905 yd; Par 72			6,506 yd; Par 72		

fairway, just a drop into the Pacific Ocean and the rugged rocks below.

The 1921 US Women's Open Champion Marion Hollins was responsible for Cypress Point after falling in love with California, and with the help of Alister Mackenzie and money donated by local businessmen her course was opened in 1928.

Mackenzie utilized the natural surroundings to the fullest but he also designed greens that added to the severity of the course; the varying contours make them extremely difficult to read.

MERION

The Merion Golf Club grew out of the Merion Cricket Club which was founded at Ardmore, Pennsylvania, in 1865. The first golf course of nine holes was laid out at nearby Haverford in 1896. It was extended to 18 holes in 1900, but it was not long enough to offer a serious test to the top golfers of the day, so a new piece of land was developed in Ardmore and the East course was opened in 1912. A second course was added two years later.

Although it had staged the US Women's Amateur Championship in 1904, it was not until after the opening of the East course that Merion became one of the great championship courses. It has now staged more US Golf Association tournaments than any other American course.

While the East course is only 6,468 yards long, designer Hugh Wilson added to Merion's severity by guarding the small greens with many bunkers. With the 2nd and 4th holes both par 5s, Merion offers as tough a start to a round of golf as any course in America.

Merion first hosted the US Open in 1934 when Olin Dutra came from eight behind after 36 holes to take the title, and it was at Merion in 1930 that Bobby Jones completed golf's greatest Grand Slam when he took the US Amateur title.

THE GREAT COURSES

MERION			MUIRFIELD VILLAGE		
Hole	Yards	Par	Hole	Yards	Par
1	362	4	1	446	4
2	536	5	2	452	4
3	181	3	3	392	4
4	600	5	4	204	3
5	418	4	5	531	5
6	420	4	6	430	4
7	350	4	7	549	5
8	360	4	8	189	3
9	179	3	9	410	4
10	310	4	10	441	4
11	369	4	11	538	5
12	371	4	12	156	3
13	127	3	13	442	4
14	408	4	14	363	4
15	366	4	15	490	5
16	428	4	16	204	3
17	220	3	17	430	4
18	463	4	18	437	4
6,468 yd; Par 70			7,104 yd; Par 72		

MUIRFIELD VILLAGE

Designed by Jack Nicklaus, Muirfield Village is named after the Scottish course that was the scene of Nicklaus' first British Open success in 1966.

Although he has helped with the design of many other courses world-wide, Nicklaus had the idea of building his own course in his home town of Columbus, Ohio, shortly after winning the 1966 Masters. When he won the British Open a couple of months later, the course found its name.

With Augusta being one of his favourite courses, Nicklaus was determined to incorporate some of the beauty of the Georgia course in his own design, and there are traits of the Masters' venue about Muirfield Village. Knowing what club and professional players alike wanted out of a golf course, Nicklaus, along with Peter Dye and Desmond Muirhead, came up with a course that can be both tough and fair. They also took into consideration the needs of golf fans,

*Previous page: The
16th hole at Cypress
point.*

and Muirfield Village is a good spectator
course, which is one reason why it was
chosen for the 1987 Ryder Cup – when in
fact the Americans lost on home soil for the
first time.

Muirfield Village opened in 1976 and since
then has played host each year to the
Memorial Tournament, one of the US Tour
events. Jack Nicklaus has won the title twice.

PEBBLE BEACH

Another course on the Monterey Peninsula,
Pebble Beach offers the same scenic
grandeur as Cypress Point and it must rank
as one of the most spectacular courses in the
United States. The 107-yard, par 3 7th at
Pebble Beach is probably the most
photographed hole in the world as the green
juts out into the Pacific and the golfer often

has to contend with waves, and fish, lapping
up on to the green during a putt.

The 8th is just as spectacular with your
second shot requiring a carry over a 100-foot
drop into the Pacific, and the par 5 18th,
along the rugged coastline, is one of the
toughest closing holes in golf. Most golfers
are grateful to make par to complete their
round. One man who bettered this at the
18th, and also the tough 17th, was Tom
Watson on his way to winning the 1982 US
Open when he made two birdies to snatch
the title from Jack Nicklaus. The course
staged two other Opens, in 1972 and 1992.

Pebble Beach was the first of the many golf
courses on this part of the Californian coast,
and was the idea of Samuel Morse, nephew of
the man who gave us Morse Code. It was
opened in 1919 and spreads from the
coastline inland to the edge of the Del
Monte Forest.

*Left: Sand, sand,
everywhere. The view
of the par 4 2nd at Pine
Valley.*

PINE VALLEY

The Pine Valley course was the vision of George Crump, owner of the Colonnades, Hotel in Philadelphia, Pennsylvania. Crump wanted to build the best and most demanding golf course in the world. He called in British designer, H.S. Colt, who developed a 184-acre forest area at Clementon, New Jersey, in order to fulfil Crump's dream.

The course was opened in 1916 and three years later its 14 holes were extended to 18. Crump's dream of making it one of the best and toughest courses in the world was realized, and it immediately gained respect from professional golfers of the day.

The countless bunkers add to Pine Valley's severity and the 367-yard, par 4 2nd hole presents one of the most daunting tasks in golf as you stand on the tee and see little else but bunkers along the fairway. A bucket and spade are probably as much use as a sand wedge on this hole! Pinpoint accuracy is required off all tees as there is hardly any room for error in finding what little bit of fairway there is at Pine Valley.

Above and left: After the difficult short 7th, the 8th at Pebble Beach offers no respite.

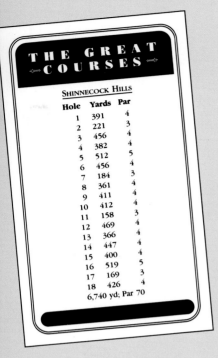

SHINNECOCK HILLS

Hole	Yards	Par
1	391	4
2	221	3
3	456	4
4	382	4
5	512	5
6	456	4
7	184	3
8	361	4
9	411	4
10	412	4
11	158	3
12	469	4
13	366	4
14	447	4
15	400	4
16	519	5
17	169	3
18	426	4

6,740 yd; Par 70

The Shinnecock Hills clubhouse.

SHINNECOCK HILLS

Shinnecock Hills is named after the tribe of Shinnecock Indians who used to live in South-eastern Long Island where the course is located. The club was formed in 1891 and is one of the oldest still-surviving clubs in America. The idea for this course came after businessman William Vanderbilt saw Scottish professional Willie Dunn play in Europe. Vanderbilt then recruited the services of Dunn to lay out the course and appointed him as the club's first professional.

America's first 18-hole course opened in 1891 and a year later, the magnificent clubhouse, designed by Stanford White, was inaugurated. The course reflected many features of the courses in Dunn's homeland.

Shinnecock Hills played host to the second US Open in 1896 but did not host its second championship until 1986 when Ray Floyd became the oldest champion at the age of 43.

The course was regarded as too short for the professionals of the 1930s and it was unlikely to be regarded as a championship course again unless it was extended, so in the 1930s Dick Wilson was called in to make major changes. It now measures 6,740 yards.

EUROPE

VALDERRAMA (SPAIN)

Spain's Costa del Sol has gained a reputation for being one of the foremost golfing centres in Europe in the last decade and Valderrama boasts one of Spain's finest, if not oldest, golf clubs. It is often referred to as 'Europe's Augusta'.

Valderrama was laid out in the picturesque Sotogrande area of Spain by top designer Robert Trent Jones in 1964 and was originally known as Los Aves. Within two years it was hosting the Spanish Open, which Argentina's Roberto de Vicenzo won.

A consortium of eight Spanish businessmen acquired the course in the mid-1980s and they decided to turn it into an exclusive golfing centre. The course was re-vamped and turned into a challenging course, testing enough to meet the demands of the 1980s golf professional, and its closing nine holes provide one of the toughest tests on the European Tour.

The Volvo Masters has its home at Valderrama, where the beautiful scenery can often detract from the job in hand; conquering a very tough golf course.

ST NOM-LA-BRÊTECHE (FRANCE)

The home of one of the Volvo Tour's top events, the Lancôme Trophy, since its launch in 1970, the St Nom-la-Brêteche course is situated close to Versailles.

The original course was designed by British designer Fred Hawtree. A second was added later and there are now two courses; the Red and the Blue. It has been used to host many domestic championships including the French Open on three occasions, the third time being in 1982 when Spain's

The closing hole at Valderrama, described as 'Spain's Augusta'.

Langer during the 1989 Lâncome Trophy, at St Nom-la-Brêteche. Langer finished second to Argentina's Eduardo Romero.

Severiano Ballesteros won the title. The first winner in 1965 was Seve's uncle, Ramon Sota. The other French Open held at St Nom-la-Brêteche, in 1969, was won by Jean Garaialde who became the first Frenchman for 22 years to win his home Open.

The Versailles course hosted the then-prestigious World Cup in 1963 when Arnold Palmer and Jack Nicklaus took the team prize for the United States with Nicklaus capturing the individual title.

THE GREAT COURSES

VALDERRAMA

Hole	Yards	Par
1	387	4
2	410	4
3	171	3
4	563	5
5	376	4
6	164	3
7	459	4
8	349	4
9	454	4
10	404	4
11	551	5
12	219	3
13	401	4
14	369	4
15	226	4
16	421	3
17	568	5
18	456	4
4,950 yd; Par 71		

ST-NOM-LA-BRÊTECHE

Hole	Yards	Par
1	364	4
2	417	4
3	188	3
4	397	4
5	486	5
6	438	4
7	509	5
8	422	4
9	209	3
10	418	4
11	373	4
12	545	5
13	214	3
14	356	4
15	396	4
16	191	3
17	509	5
18	363	4
5,680 yd; Par 72		

PENINA (PORTUGAL)

Think of Penina and you think of one man: Henry Cotton. It was after retiring to Portugal when his playing days were over that the three-times British Open champion developed the Penina golf course and his famous golfing school.

The climate makes Penina a popular venue with tourists and aspiring professionals and each autumn the PGA takes young hopefuls to Penina to carry on the tradition started by Cotton, who died in 1987. The magnificent Penina hotel, which dominates the skyline adjacent to the course, regularly has 'full' notices posted. Developed in 1964 on flat land in his beloved Algarve area of Portugal, Cotton planted over thousands of trees to transform a waterlogged field into a beautiful golf course.

The inward nine holes at Penina offer some of the toughest golf in Europe and the last nine holes start and finish with two par 5s, thus making the inward par of 38 a difficult target. But Cotton's course is as fair as it is tough, and pre-planning at every hole is important. The foolhardy will find themselves paying for their mistakes.

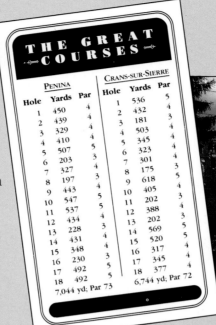

THE GREAT COURSES

	PENINA			CRANS-SUR-SIERRE	
Hole	Yards	Par	Hole	Yards	Par
1	450	4	1	536	5
2	439	4	2	432	4
3	329	4	3	181	3
4	410	4	4	503	4
5	507	5	5	345	4
6	203	3	6	323	4
7	327	4	7	301	4
8	197	3	8	175	3
9	443	4	9	618	5
10	547	5	10	405	4
11	537	5	11	202	3
12	434	4	12	388	4
13	228	3	13	202	3
14	431	4	14	569	5
15	348	4	15	520	5
16	230	3	16	317	4
17	492	5	17	345	4
18	492	5	18	377	4
7,044 yd; Par 73			6,744 yd; Par 72		

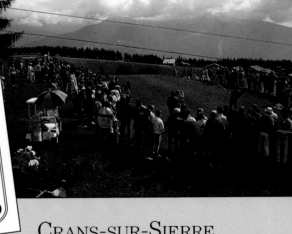

Above: Action from the 1989 European Masters-Swiss Open at Crans-sur-Sierre. Ballesteros won his third Swiss Open.

The 9th at Penina.

CRANS-SUR-SIERRE (SWITZERLAND)

For a spectacular setting, Switzerland's Crans-sur-Sierre course, with the backdrop of the Matterhorn, takes some beating.

Situated 5,000 feet above the Rhône Valley, the original course was laid out by skiing holiday pioneer Sir Arnold Lunn in 1905 after he had already built the nearby Palace Hotel. However, tourists did not come to Switzerland to play golf, preferring the skiing *pistes*, and the golf course closed during World War I.

Attempts to re-open the course failed in the early 1920s but in 1927 the current course was opened and golf in the area has grown in popularity since then.

The Swiss Open has been played at Crans since 1939 and it was during the 1961 Open that Italy's Baldovino Dassu shot a European Tour 18-hole record 60. And in the 1978 Open Spain's José-Maria Olazabal shot a European Tour 9-hole record 27.

It is the largest club in Switzerland but the snow-covered fairways necessitate its closure in the winter months. The rarified atmosphere often makes the club golfer feel like Ian Woosnam, Sandy Lyle or Greg Norman off the tee.

AROUND THE WORLD

ROYAL MELBOURNE (AUSTRALIA)

Royal Melbourne offers the golfer a mixture of Augusta's beauty, and the characteristics of many of the Scottish links courses. It is one of the great championship courses outside Britain and America.

The first course was laid out in 1891 and has had constant membership since that date. The course moved from its original site to the Sandringham area of Melbourne in 1901 and in the 1920s Alister Mackenzie was called in to redesign Royal Melbourne. As he assisted with the design of Augusta, it is hardly surprising that there are similarities to the Georgia course.

A second course, the East course, was added in 1932 and such is the design of the two that holes from both can be incorporated into one 18-hole championship course as and when needed.

The greens are very fast because they are relaid every five or six years, and at the 6th and 14th holes the amateur and professional golfer alike is faced with two testing dog-legs which both require correct club selection, followed by an accurate drive.

Royal Melbourne hosted the World Cup in 1959 when Peter Thomson and Kel Nagle provided home winners. When it was played at Royal Melbourne again in 1972 Taiwan were the surprise victors.

The 6th hole at Royal Melbourne.

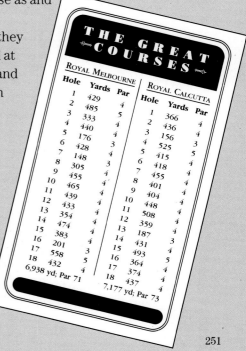

THE GREAT COURSES

ROYAL MELBOURNE			ROYAL CALCUTTA		
Hole	Yards	Par	Hole	Yards	Par
1	429	4			
2	485	5	1	366	4
3	333	4	2	436	4
4	440	4	3	156	3
5	176	3	4	525	5
6	428	4	5	415	4
7	148	3	6	418	4
8	305	4	7	455	4
9	455	4	8	401	4
10	465	4	9	404	4
11	439	4	10	448	4
12	433	4	11	508	5
13	354	4	12	359	4
14	474	4	13	187	4
15	383	4	14	431	4
16	201	4	15	493	5
17	558	3	16	364	5
18	432	4	17	374	4
6,938 yd; Par 71			18	437	4
			7,177 yd; Par 73		

ROYAL CALCUTTA (INDIA)

Formed in 1829, the Royal Calcutta Club is the oldest club outside Britain, and the Indian Amateur Championship, which has been held at the course since 1892, is one of the oldest championships in the world. The club received 'Royal' patronage from King George V in 1911.

The original course was laid out in the Dum Dum area of Calcutta, where Calcutta's international airport is now situated. The club moved to the Tollygunge area of Calcutta and over the years the site, which was once a paddy-field, has been developed into one of the great golf courses of the world with plant and tree life being nurtured to a high standard.

To the uninitiated, the course looks easy; but it is not. The par 4s are deceptive, and require good iron play off the fairways, and the small greens are filled with hidden rolls and undulations.

GLEN ABBEY (CANADA)

The home of the Royal Canadian Golf Association, Glen Abbey was one of the first purpose-built golf courses to meet the excessive demands of golf in the boom years of the 1970s.

Jack Nicklaus was asked to assist with the design and he took full advantage of the natural features of the area close to Lake Ontario in the Oakville district of Ontario.

As with his own Muirfield Village course, Nicklaus gave consideration to the spectator as well as providing a tough test for the golfer. The large pedestrian areas between fairways, and banked areas behind the greens, are testament to Nicklaus' conception.

Jack Nicklaus, who assisted in the design of Glen Abbey.

Nicklaus did not have to start from scratch, because a course had been laid out in the 1960s, but his task was a major rebuilding one designed to take the course into the 1970s and beyond. He has certainly done that, and with the exception of 1980, Glen Abbey has been the permanent home of the Canadian Open since 1977, the year after it opened.

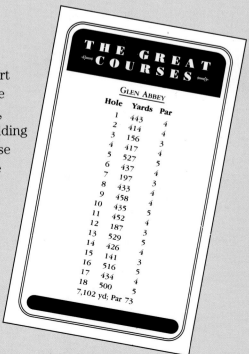

THE GREAT COURSES

GLEN ABBEY

Hole	Yards	Par
1	443	4
2	414	4
3	156	3
4	417	4
5	527	5
6	437	4
7	197	3
8	433	4
9	458	4
10	435	5
11	452	4
12	187	3
13	529	5
14	426	4
15	141	3
16	516	5
17	434	4
18	500	5

7,102 yd; Par 73

GLOSSARY

Address   The position that the player stands in before making the swing.

Air Shot   This is a complete miss.

Albatross   British term used when your score is three below the par of the hole. In America this is known as a double eagle.

Approach Shots   Shots played to the green from the fairway, with medium or short clubs.

Birdie   Term used when your score is one below the par of the hole.

Blind Hole   A hole where the player cannot see the green or flagstick when playing the hole.

Bogey   Term used when your score is one stroke over the par of a hole.

Borrow   British term for the amount you have to allow for a putt to move from a straight line due to the slope of a green.

Break   American term for the amount you have to allow for a putt to move from a straight line due to the slope of a green.

Bunker   A hole in the ground filled with sand.

Carry   The distance the ball flies through the air.

Closed Stance   When a line across the feet at the address points to the right of the intended target.

Cup   The lining inside the hole, normally made of metal or plastic.

Divot   A divot is the turf removed by the clubhead when a stroke is played.

Dog-leg Hole   A hole that curves either left to right, or right to left, from the tee to the green.

Drive   A shot played from the teeing surface.

Fairway   The closely mown area between the tee and the green.

Green   The area of closely mown grass prepared for putting, with the hole cut into it.

Grounding the Club   This is when the clubhead is allowed to lie on the ground.

Lie   This describes the position of the ball. It also refers to the angle of the shaft of the club from the sole of the club.

Loft   The angle on the face of each club.

Plugged Ball   A ball remaining in its own indentation when landing on soft ground, or in a bunker.

Preferred Lies   Sometimes due to bad weather conditions the player is allowed to clean and replace their ball when on the fairway.

Rookie   The name given to a Tour player who is in their first year.

Rough   All ground that is not mown for the tee, fairway, green or hazard.

Teeing Ground   A prepared area from which each hole is started.

Tee Peg   A means of raising the ball above the ground when the first stroke is played from the teeing ground.

Tony Jacklin

INDEX

Page numbers in *italic* refer to illustrations

A
address, putting, 84
Alcott, Amy, 5, 206, *206*
Alliss, Percy, 239
Alliss, Peter, 235
Anderson, Jamie, 208
Anderson, Jessie, 222
Anderson, Willie, 212
Armour, Tommy, 217, 238
arms, warm-up exercises, 59
Asian Tour, 232
Augusta, 184, 192, *242*
Australian Tour, 229
Azinger, Paul, 197

B
backswing, 46
Baker-Finch, Ian, 211, *211*, 229,
    229, 236
Balata balls, 14
ball:
    dropping, 160
    falling off tee peg, 159
    flight-path, 56
    lost, 160
    out of bounds, 160
    in play, 159–60
    playing the wrong one, 160
    position, 35
    teeing-up, 21
    unfit for play, 160
Ball, John, 224, *224, 254*
ball-to-target line, 24
    putting, 84
Ballesteros, Baldomero, 195
Ballesteros, Manuel, 195
Ballesteros, Severiano, *37, 123*,
    195, *195*, 198, *210*, 211, 216, 219
    236, 237, 249
Ballesteros, Vicente, 195

John Ball driving.

balls, 14–15
    Balata, 14
    dimpled, 171
    evolution, 170–1
    feathery, 170–1, *170*
    guttapercha, *170*, 171
    Haskell, 171
    three-piece, 15
    two-piece, 15, 16, *16*, 170, *171*
Barnes, Jim, 181, 217, *217*
Bean, Andy, 194
Belfry, 235, *235*
Belgian Open, 185
Beman, Deane, 226
Benson & Hedges Masters, 199
Bent Tree Ladies' Classic, 205
Berg, Patty, 227
Berrie, J.A.A., 184
Black, John, 213
Bob Hope Desert Classic, 190
body alignment, 33
Bonallack, Michael, 221, 226
Bradley, Pat, 204, *204*, 227, *233*
Bradshaw, Harry, 188
Braid, James, 178, *178*, 180, *180*,
    181, 209, 218, 239
Brand, Gordon jr, 199
Brewer, Gay, 215
British Amateur Championship,
    224–6
British Open Championship:
    early years, 177, 178, 179, 180,
        181, 183, 184, 185, 208–9
    first, *169*, 175, 176
    history, 208–11
    post-war, 185, 186, 188, 189,
        190, 191, 192, 193, 194, 195,
        196, 197, 198, 199, 209–11
Broadstone, Sir Thomas, 167
Brookline, 181, *181*
Brown, George, 208
Brown, Michael, *169, 208*
bunkers, 161
    fairway, 100–2
    greenside, 92–9
Burns, George, 213

C
Cacharel Under-25s
    Championship, 198
Calcavecchia, Mark, *155*, 211
Calcutta Club, 168
Canadian Open, 190, 193, 199
Carner, JoAnne, 203
Carnoustie, 180, 185, 191, 194, 238,
    238
Casper, Billy, *190*, 214
casual water, 161
cavity-back clubs, *9*, 173, *173*
Charles, Bob, 191, 210, 237
chipping, 75–9
    errors, 141–3
clothing, cold weather, 17
    rain, 18
clubs, 9–18
    aiming, 20–4
    distance, 12, *12–13*
    evolution, 172–3
    grip, 11, 18
    half-sets, 10, *10*
    hand-made, *17*
    head, 20
    hooded, *75*
    lie of, 21
    loft, 12
    open and closed faces, 22–3,
        22–3
    shafts, 10
    swing weighting, 11
    in the wet, 18
colf, 167
Colt, H.S., 247
Compston, Archie, 181
Cook, John, 226, *226*
Cotton, Henry, 185, *185*, 209, 211,
    239, 250
Couples, Fred, 53, *156*, 216, *216*
courses, 18-hole standard, 168
Crail Golfing Club, 168
Crans-sur-Sierre, 250, *250*
Crenshaw, Ben, 195, 211
Crump, George, 247
Curtis, Harriot, 222, *222*
Curtis, Margaret, 222, *222*
Curtis Cup, 222
Cypress Point, 242, *243, 244*

D
Daly, Fred, 185, 209
Daniel, Beth, 204
Dassu, Baldovino, 250
Davies, Laura, 233, *233*
Deal, 178
Devlin, Bruce, 223
Diegel, Leo, 209
difficult lies, 91–114
    ball above feet, 108–9
    ball below feet, 106–7
    downhill, 105
    in bushes, 112
    over trees, 110
    under trees, 112–13
    uphill, 104

downhill lies, 105
downswing, 50–3
Du Maurier Classic, 204, 206, 227
Duncan, George, 219
Dunhill Cup, *196*
Dunlop Masters, 191, 199
Dunn, Jamie, 175
Dunn, Willie, 175, 247
Dutra, Olin, 243
Dye, Peter, 243

E
Edinburgh Golfing Society, 167
Eisenhower, President Dwight D.,
    223
Eisenhower Trophy, 222–3
English Amateur Championship,
    197
equipment, 9–18
    balls, 14–15, 170–1
    clubs, 9–14, 172–3
    history, 170–3
Espinosa, Al, 184

F
fairway bunkers, 100–2
Faldo, Nick, 5, 74, *103*, 197, *197*,
    209, 211, 216, *232*, 239, *255*
faults, 115–34
    chipping errors, 141–3
    fluffing, 129–31
    hooking, 120–2
    over-swinging, 132–5
    pitching errors, 136–40
    pulling, 119, 122
    pushing, 122, 124–5
    putting errors, 141–151
    slicing, 116–18, 122
    topping, 126–8
Fazio, George, 214
feathery golf balls, 170–1, *170*
Federal Express St Jude Classic,
    196
Ferguson, Bob, 208
Flanders, 166
flight path, 56
Floyd, Ray, 198, 199, 248
fluffing, 129–31
    pitching, 138
four ball, 154
foursome, 153
    handicaps, 157
full swing, 38–9

G
Ganton, 181
Garaialde, Jean, 249
Garrido, Antonio, 219
Gentleman Golfers of Edinburgh,
    167
German Open, 198
Girl Talk Classic, 204
Glen Abbey, 252
Gleneagles, 180, 239, *239*

Gloucester golfer window, 167, *167*
golf balls *see* balls
Grady, Wayne, 217
Graham, David, 213, 217, 229
Great Triumvirate, 178–80
Green, Hubert, 213
greens, rules, 162–3
Greensboro Open, 186
greenside bunkers, 92–9
    ball back in, 95
    ball on firm sand, 97
    ball on up-slope, 98
    ball plugged in, 99
    ball sat down, 96
grip, 25–31
    ball alignment, 44–5
    common faults, 30–1
    left hand, 25
    pressure, 28
    putting, 83
    right hand, 26
    women, 29
    young players, 29
grips, 10
    wet, 18
ground under repair, 161
Guldahl, Ralph, 248

H
Hagen, Walter, 182, *182*, 209, *209*, 213, 217, 218, 228
handicaps, 156–7
hands, warm-up exercises, 59
Hanson, Beverley, 227
Harwood, Mike, *229*
Haskell, Coburn, 171
Haskell golf ball, 171
Havers, Arthur, 182
Hawtree, Fred, 249
Hayes, Mark, 185
hazards, 91–114, 161–2
Hazeltine, 205
Herd, Sandy, 171, 180
Hershey Four ball, 187
Hill, Mike, 232
Hilton, Harold, 224, 239
Hilton Head, 198
hips, warm-up exercises, 61
history, 166–233
Hogan, Ben, 186, 187, *187*, 208, 212, *213*, 214, 215, 238, 239, 248
Hollins, Marion, 242
Homans, Eugene, 184
honour, 158
hooded club, 75
hooking, 120–2
Hoylake, 180, 184, 189, 208
Huggett, Brian, 189
Hutchinson, Horace, 224
Hutchison, Jock, 209, 217
Hyndman, Bill, 223

I
inside ground, 54
Inverness Club, Ohio, 181
Irwin, Hale, 194, 213

J
Jack, Reid, 223
Jacklin, Tony, 210, 212, *213*, 220,

220, 235, 237, 240, *253*
Jacobs, John, 229
Jacobs, Tommy, 215
James IV, King of Scotland, 167, *167*
Jameson, Betty, 227
Jones, Bobby, 180, 184, *184*, 209, 212, 213, 214–15, 221, 224, 226, 228, 237, 242, 243
Jones, Robert Trent, 249
Jones, Rolland, 180

K
Kemper Open, 199
Kentucky Derby Open, 191
Kite, Tom, 196, *196*, 213, 216
Knight, Ray, 205

L
La Grange, 204
Ladies' Professional Golf Association (LPGA), 233
Langer, Bernhard, *84*, *147*, 195, 198, *198*, 216, 220
Langley Park, 185
Leadbetter, David, 197, *255*
legs, warm-up exercises, 61
Lema, Tony, 215
Little, Lawson, 226
Littler, Gene, 226
Locke, Bobby, 188, *188*, 189, *189*, 209, 237
long putt, 86
Lopez, Nancy, *38*, 205, *205*
Los Angeles Open, 17
Lunn, Sir Arnold, 250
Lyle, Sandy, *114*, 210, 211, *211*, 216, 250
Lytham and St Anne's, 188, 189, 191, 195, *237*

M
Macdonald, Charles, 226
McDermott, Johnny, 212
McFie, Allan, 224
Mackenzie, Alister, 215, 242, 251
Mallon, Meg, *233*
Mangrum, Lloyd, 214
Mansell, Nigel, *199*
Martini International, 199
Mary, Queen of Scots, 167
Massy, Arnaud, 179
match-play, 153
    handicaps, 157
matches, types, 153
medium swing, 40–1
Merion, 184, 187, 243
Miller, Johnny, 195, 213, 215, 236
Mitchell, Abe, 218
Mochrie, Dottie, *43*
Monastir, *157*
Morris, Old Tom, 170, 175, 176, *176*, *177*, 208, 239
Morris, Young Tom, 170, 177, *177*, 208
Morse, Samuel, 246
Muirfield, 178, 180, 181, 185, 192, 193, 194, 197, 208, 239–40, 243–4
Muirhead, Desmond, 243
Musselburgh, 177

N
Nabisco Dinah Shore, 204, 206, 227
Nagle, Kel, 191, 209, 251
Nelson, Byron, 186
Nelson, Harry, 213
Newton, Jack, 194, 211, 238
Nicholas, Allison, *233*
Nicklaus, Jack, 186, 190, 191, 192, *192*, 194, 195, 196, 199, 208, 210, 211, 212, *214*, 215–16, 220, 223, 226, 232, 239–40, 243, 246, 248, 249, 252, *252*
Norman, Greg, *49*, 199, *199*, 211, 216, 229, 250
North, Andy, 213
North Berwick, 175, 177

O
Oak Hill, 193
Oakhurst Club, 169
Oakmont, 192
O'Connor, Christy, 189
Olazabal, José-Maria, 226, 250
O'Meara, Mark, 226
Oosterhuis, Peter, 191
Orange Blossom Classic, 206
origins of golf, 166–73
Ouimet, Francis, 179, 181, *181*, 212, *212*
outside ground, 54
over-swinging, 132–5

P
Palmer, Arnold, *30*, 190, *190*, 209–10, *209*, 214, *214*, 215, 217, *223*, 226, 232, 236, 248, 249
Park, Mungo, 177
Park, Willie, 169, 176, 208, *208*
Pate, Jerry, 213, 223, 226
Pau, 168, *169*
Pavin, Corey, 232
Pebble Beach, 194, 196, *230*, 246, *246*

Penina, 250, *250*
Peter Jackson Classic, 204, 206, 227
Pine Valley, 247, *247*
pitching, 60–74
    errors, 136–40
    correct pitch, 140
    fluffing, 138
    short high lob shots, 70
    short pitches, 68
    socket, 139–40
    topping, 136–7
pitching wedge, 71–4
Player, Gary, 190, 191, *191*, 208, 209, 210, 215, 217, 232, 237
posture, 34
Potter, Thomas Owen, 224
pressure shots, 60
Preston, Robert, 171
Prestwick, 169, *169*, 176, 177, 179, 181, 208
Price, Nick, 217, *217*, 232
Professional Golfers Association (PGA), 178
pulling, 119, 122
pushing, 122, 124–5
putter heads, *9*
putting, 80–90
    address, 84
    ball alignment, 82
    ball-target line, 84
    errors, 141–51
    grip, 83
    long putt, 86
    practice, 87
    shaping, 90
    short putt, 85

R
rain, playing in, 18
Rawlins, Horace, 169, 212
Rawls, Betsy, 227
Ray, Ted, 181, 212, 218
Rees, Dai, 219, *219*

Robertson, Allan, 169, 170, 175, *175*, 176, *176*
Rogers, Bill, 198, 213
Royal and Ancient, 167–8, 189, 224
Royal Birkdale, 189, 193, 194, 195, 236, *236*
Royal Blackheath Club, 168, 180
Royal Burgess Golfing Society of Edinburgh, 167
Royal Calcutta Club, 168, 252
Royal Melbourne, 251
Royal Mid-Surrey Club, 178
rules, 158–63
Ryder, Samuel, 218
Ryder Cup, 169, 181, 185, 192, 193, 195, *195*, 197, *200*

S
Safari Tour, 229
St Andrews, 167, 176, 178, 179, 180, 184, 186, 188, 195, 197, 208, 240–1, *240*

St Nom-La Brêteche, *8*, 249, *249*
Sands, C.E., 226
Sandwich, 178, 179, 185, 188, 208
Sarazen, Gene, 183, *183*, 208, 213, 215, 217, 228
Scheldt, *169*
score card, 154
    Royal Birkdale, *154*
Sea Pines Heritage Classic, 197, 198
shafts, materials, 172–3
shaping, putting, 90
Sheehan, Patty, 227, *227*
Shinnecock Hills, 199, 248, *248*
Shirley, Jean, 201
short game, 60–79
    chipping, 75–9
    pitching, 60–75
short putt, 85
short swing, 40–1
shoulders, warm-up exercises, 60
slicing, 116–18, 122
sloping lies, 107–9
Smith, Horton, 215, *215*
Smith, Macdonald, 209

Snead, Sam, 186, *186*, 209, 213, 215, 217, *219*, 239
socket, pitching errors, 139–40
Solheim, Karsten, *203*

spliced-head drivers, *10*
square set-up, 34
stableford, 153
    handicaps, 157
Stadler, Craig, 226
stance, 32–7
    ball position, 35
    body alignment, 33
    posture, 34
starting out, 19–64
State Express Classic, 199
Stewart, Payne, 1
Strange, Curtis, *48*, 198, 213
stretching exercises, 64–5
stroke-play, 153
    handicaps, 157
Suggs, Louise, 227
Sunshine Tour, 232
Sutton, Hal, *223*
swing, 38–58
    backswing, 47
    downswing, 50–3
    full swing, 38–9
    grip and ball alignment, 44–5
    medium swing, 40–1
    short swing, 40–1
    swing path, 54–8
    takeaway, 46
    warm-up exercises, 62–3
    women, 42–3

T
takeaway, 46
Taylor, John Henry, 178, *178*, 179, 180, 181, 208–9, 218
teeing ground, 158–9
thinning *see* topping
Thomas, Dave, 189, 235
Thomson, Peter, 188, 189, *189*, 194, 209, 236, 237, 251
three-piece balls, 15, *15*
topping, 126–8
    pitching, 136–7
tours, 228–33
Transvaal Open, 188
trees:
    high shots over, 110–11
    low shots under, 112–13
Trevino, Lee, 190, 193, *193*, 232, 236, 240
Troon, 182, 183, 188, 194
Turnberry, 185, *192*, 194, *194*, 199, *241*
Turnesa, Jim, 186
Tway, Bob, 199

U
uphill lies, 104
US Amateur Championship, 190, 192, 196, 226
US Golf Association, 169
US LPGA Championship, 227
US LPGA Tour, 233
US Masters, 183, 184, 186, 187, 190, 191, 192, 195
    history, 214–16
US Open Championship:

early, 169, 179, 181, 182, 183, 184, 186, 212–13
    history, 212–14
    post-war, 187, 188, 190, 191, 192, 193, 194, 196, 199, 213
US PGA Championship, 182, 183, 186, 187, 190, 191, 192, 193, 199
    history, 217
US PGA Seniors' Tour, 232
US PGA Tour, 228
US Women's Open, 201–6, 227

V
Valderrama, *234*, 249, *249*
Vanderbilt, William, 247
Vardon, Harry, *28*, 170, 178, *178*, 179, *179*, 180, 181, *181*, 209, 212, 218
Verulam Golf Club, 218
Vicenzo, Roberto de, 188, 249
Virginia Closed Championship, 186
Volpe, Ray, 233
Volvo Tour, 228–9

W
Wadkins, Bobby, 198
Wadkins, Lanny, 226, *226*
Walker, George, 223
Walker, Herbert, 221
Walker Cup, 169, 196, 220–1
Wallace, Jack, 226
warm-up exercises, 59–64
    arms, 59
    hands, 59
    hips, 61
    legs, 61
    shoulders, 60
    stretching, 64–5
    swing, 62–3
water:
    casual, 161
    on the green, 163
    hazards, 162
    lateral hazards, 162
Waterloo Club, 185
Watson, Tom, 194, *194*, 195, 210–11, 236, 238, 246
Weiskopf, Tom, 215
Wentworth, 191, 238–9, *238*
Western Open, 194
Westward Ho! Golf Club, 178
Wheeler, Frank, 218
White, Stanford, 248
Whitworth, Kathy, 203, *203*
Wilson, Dick, 248
Wilson, Hugh, 243
Winged Foot, 184
women:
    championships, 227
    famous players, 201–6
    grip, 29
    swing, 42–3
    tours, 233
Women's European Tour, 233

wooden clubs, 172–3

Wright, Mickey, 202, *202*, 227, *227*

Z
Zaharias, Mildred, 201, *201*
Zoeller, Fuzzy, 213

The Master's flag.